NEW YORK REVIEW BOOKS
CLASSICS

THE BURNING OF THE WORLD

BÉLA ZOMBORY-MOLDOVÁN (1885–1967) was born in
Munkács (now Mukachevo), in what was then the Kingdom
of Hungary, part of the Austro-Hungarian Empire. After
graduating from the Academy of Fine Arts in Budapest, he
established himself as a painter, illustrator, and graphic artist.
Wounded in action in 1914 as a junior officer on the eastern
front, he served the rest of the First World War in non-
combatant duties. He was a successful painter, especially of
portraits, during the interwar years, and was the principal
of the Budapest School of Applied Arts from 1935 until his
dismissal by the Communist regime in 1946. Out of official
favor and artistic fashion in the postwar years, he devoted
himself to the quiet landscapes in oils and watercolor that
are his finest work. The writing of his recently discovered
memoirs probably also dates from those years of seclusion.

PETER ZOMBORY-MOLDOVAN has co-translated Arthur
Schnitzler's *Reigen* and is working on a new version of Bertolt
Brecht's *Furcht und Elend des Dritten Reiches* for the English
stage. A grandson of Béla Zombory-Moldován, he lives in
London.

Béla Zombory-Moldován, *Self-portrait*, 1915. Graphite pencil.

The collar insignia denote the rank of second lieutenant of the Austro-Hungarian infantry.

THE BURNING OF THE WORLD
A Memoir of 1914

BÉLA ZOMBORY-MOLDOVÁN

*Translated from the Hungarian and
with an introduction and notes by*
PETER ZOMBORY-MOLDOVAN

NEW YORK REVIEW BOOKS

New York

THIS IS A NEW YORK REVIEW BOOK
PUBLISHED BY THE NEW YORK REVIEW OF BOOKS
435 Hudson Street, New York, NY 10014
www.nyrb.com

Maps: Ted McGrath

Zombory-Moldován, Béla, 1885–1967.
 The burning of the world : a memoir of 1914 / by Béla Zombory-Moldován ;
translated from the Hungarian by Peter Zombory-Moldovan.
     pages cm — (New York Review Books classics)
 ISBN 978-1-59017-809-6 (paperback)
 1. Zombory-Moldován, Béla, 1885–1967. 2. World War, 1914–1918—Personal
narratives, Hungarian. 3. World War, 1914–1918—Social aspects—Hungary.
4. Soldiers—Hungary—Biography. 5. Veterans—Hungary—Biography. 6.
Artists—Hungary—Biography. 7. Hungary—History—1867–1918—Biography.
I. Zombory-Moldovan, Peter. II. Title.
 D640.Z64 2014
 940.4'13439092—dc23
 [B]

                    2014013207

ISBN 978-1-59017-809-6
Available as an electronic book; ISBN 978-1-59017-810-2

Printed in the United States of America on acid-free paper.
10 9 8 7 6 5 4 3 2 1

CONTENTS

A page from the autograph manuscript of *The Burning of the World*.

The text is from chapter 7 and corresponds with the passage on page 72 beginning "Then he gathered himself together" in the second paragraph and ending "Yes, far away" in the penultimate paragraph.

INTRODUCTION

SUMMER. Friends pose for a photograph on a beach. They are tanned and at ease in their outfits of white linen and cotton. The men cover their heads against the bright sun, the women wear their hair bobbed or tied back. They look in the prime of life, mostly in their late twenties or early thirties: young professionals (lawyers, publishers, teachers, a couple of artists) on a group holiday at the Mediterranean coast. They smile or gaze at the view; a small child in its mother's lap waves to the camera. The photographer—no doubt a local, working the beach during the season—has carefully inscribed the plate with his reference number and the date: 25/vii/1914.

The beach is at Novi Vinodolski, on the Adriatic. The confident man of twenty-nine sitting at the bottom of the photograph is my grandfather Béla Zombory-Moldován, a young artist oblivious to the fact that his carefree holiday is about to be cut short. In three days his country, Austria-Hungary, will be at war. A week from now he will be in uniform, and in just over a month he will be a thousand kilometers away, watching in horror as his comrades are torn apart by Russian artillery in the forests of Galicia.

Béla's birthplace, on April 20, 1885, was the small and ancient city of Munkács, in the foothills of the Carpathian Mountains. It lay in the east of what was then the Kingdom of Hungary, part of the Austro-Hungarian dual monarchy ruled by Franz Joseph I, the emperor of Austria and holy apostolic king of Hungary.

The Carpathians are still there. All the rest is gone.

The city continues to exist in a physical sense, but these days it is called Mukachevo, and after a thousand years, give or take, within the former Kingdom of Hungary, eighteen in the former Czechoslovakia, and forty-six in the former USSR, it is now in Ukraine. These have not been merely changes of administration. In 1910, three-quarters of its inhabitants were native speakers of Hungarian;[1] in 2001, fewer than one in ten were.

Hungary would remain a kingdom until 1946, but in name only. A short-lived Communist revolution in 1919 gave way to a nationalist regime under Admiral Miklós Horthy, who installed himself as "regent" whilst conniving in the removal from Hungary of Franz Joseph's successor, Karl. This was against the background of Hungary's dismemberment under the Treaty of Trianon of 1920, imposed by the victors of the First World War, in which the country was shorn of almost three-quarters of its prewar territory, two-thirds of its prewar population, and five of its ten largest cities. Having lost, among other things, its access to the sea at the Adriatic port of Fiume (now Rijeka), Hungary became (as one wag put it) a kingdom without a king, ruled by an admiral without a fleet. Worse was to come in 1944 and after.

This remarkable memoir—published here for the first time in any language—is a record, through the eyes of one man caught up in the maelstrom, of the fateful year when everything fell apart.

Three centuries of subjugation—first to the Ottoman Turks, then to Austria—had stoked a spirit of nationalism in Hungary, which erupted into revolution against Hapsburg rule in 1848. That revolution was suppressed; but by the Compromise of 1867, Hungary was granted home rule and (at least in principle) equal status with Austria in what was henceforth known as the dual monarchy. Hungary now had its own parliament, government, and institutions of statehood;

---

1. Of these, well over half were Jews, deported to Auschwitz by the Hungarian authorities, who were in charge again from 1939 to 1944.

only its foreign policy and defense were controlled from Vienna, which became the joint capital with Budapest. The Kingdom of Hungary then extended over a land area almost equal to that of today's Germany; it stretched from the Adriatic coast to the Tatra mountains in the north, and from what is now the Austrian district of Burgenland in the west to Transylvania in the far southeast.

An efficient railway system soon extended to the farthest reaches of the empire. The decades of stability after 1867 saw a sustained economic boom in which industry, trade, and construction took off at a rapid rate—above all, in Budapest, which was formed in 1873 with the unification of the twin cities of the ancient Buda on the west bank of the Danube and the vigorously expanding modern Pest on its east bank. This confident new metropolis built the world's second underground railway system, public buildings that rivaled (and, in the case of the vast neo-Gothic parliament building, surpassed) those of Vienna in magnificence, and entire quarters of well-appointed and elegant apartment buildings to house the mushrooming bourgeoisie and their servants.

Three sections of society, in particular, enjoyed the fruits of this age of national confidence and economic growth. The first was the aristocracy of great landowning magnates, whose economic interests were assiduously protected (largely at the expense of the peasantry) by successive governments. The second was the gentry,[2] a class of particular prominence in Hungary, large numbers of whom moved from genteel impecuniosity in the provinces to populate the new national political class, or (as in the case of Béla's father) to take up suitably gentlemanly appointments in the burgeoning civil service. Perhaps the most notable and visible beneficiaries were Hungarian Jews, who were granted equal civil and political rights in 1867. The

2. Defined with precision by Bryan Cartledge as "the upper stratum of the lesser nobility" in *The Will to Survive: A History of Hungary* (London: Timewell Press, 2006), chapter 6, n3. It has been estimated that half of all Magyars who were not servants or peasants could claim a title of nobility; see William M. Johnston, *The Austrian Mind: An Intellectual and Social History 1848–1938* (Berkeley: University of California Press, 1972), 337.

decades of political liberalism and religious tolerance that followed saw the emergence of a mainly Jewish urban upper middle class that was prominent in industry, business, the professions, and the intelligentsia.

When, in old age, people of my grandparents' generation referred to "peacetime" (*a béke*), it was to this pre-1914 period, rather than to the years between the wars, that they looked back with the keenest nostalgia. The reality is that the final decades of the monarchy were no long halcyon summer, any more than was the Edwardian age later so mythologized in the English-speaking world. Prewar Hungary was, in many respects, a troubled polity. A quarter of the population were landless peasants, trapped in abject neo-feudal servitude scarcely distinguishable from serfdom; a law of 1898 permitted owners of large estates to practice corporal punishment on agricultural workers who went on strike and to resort to press-gangs at harvest time, and the threat of starvation was never far away. Meanwhile, the growing urban proletariat endured working and living conditions far worse than those of their western European counterparts, sometimes bordering on destitution. By 1914, the stirrings of political unrest and radicalism, though routinely suppressed, were hard to ignore.

The greatest political tension in pre-1914 Austria-Hungary, however, stemmed from the refusal of the Magyar (the ethnically Hungarian) political establishment to meet the aspirations of the kingdom's minority nationalities—especially the Slovaks in the north, the Serbs in the south, and the Romanians in the southeast—to a measure of cultural and political autonomy. Hungarians were fearful of becoming outnumbered in their own country, of losing their privileged position within the empire, and, worst of all, of the prospect of the historic Magyar lands being parceled out among the various nationalities that had settled in them, mainly after Magyar depopulation during the Turkish occupation. These fears caused Budapest vigorously to resist the idea, gaining ground in Vienna, that the only stable future for an increasingly fissile empire would be some kind of multinational confederation. Hungarian governments insisted, instead, on a policy of "Magyarization"—the use of the Hungarian language (which is linguistically unrelated to the Slavic languages spoken by most of the kingdom's other nationalities) in all schools and for official business. This intransigence provoked increasing resentment and, eventually, calls for full independence among some of the minority groups. There was a growing sense of crisis as such demands received support and encouragement from neighboring states such as Romania and—as it turned out, fatefully—Serbia, with the backing of its fellow-Slav patron, Russia.

Then there was the nagging question of the future of the monarchy itself. Franz Joseph, on the throne since 1848, was held in general affection as the paternalistic guarantor of Hungary's privileged place in the empire; but he was about to turn eighty-five, and even he would not live forever. That his heir, the archduke Franz Ferdinand (shortly to visit the recently annexed province of Bosnia-Herzegovina and its capital, Sarajevo), loathed all Hungarians was a poorly kept secret. What would the future hold for Hungary once the shrewd old patriarch of the "brotherhood of nations" was gone?

Such anxieties simmered just below a surface of apparent stability and confidence in material progress. Cultural and intellectual life in Budapest—a city widely admired for its elegance and modernity—was in vigorous ferment; it was centered on Pest's many and famous coffeehouses, some of which, like the one called the New York, were of glittering magnificence.[3] Artists, writers, journalists, actors, boulevardiers, and hangers-on (overwhelmingly, but not exclusively, male) occupied regular tables, sometimes all day and late into the night, where conversation, debate, gossip, and badinage flowed freely. In an age when most unmarried men lived with their parents, it was a familiar, convivial place to meet friends; for family men it offered a refuge from domesticity for a brandy, a cigar, and a game of

---

3. For a rich and detailed evocation of this culture, see John Lukacs, *Budapest 1900: A Historical Portrait of a City and Its Culture* (New York: Grove Press, 1988).

chess. Newspaper articles and sometimes entire novels were written at corner tables, literary journals were edited and the occasional revolution was planned amid the clink of espresso cups. For those in search of fresh air and a refreshing spritzer or cold beer, charming old taverns in the hills of Buda offered outdoor tables under the welcoming shade of trees.

The *Sezession* style in architecture and design of the turn of the century, which had recently left its distinctive, faintly exotic mark all over Pest, was being superseded by the first waves of twentieth-century modernism in the visual arts: fauvism, cubism, expression-ism—a dizzying torrent of "isms" that stirred intense debate and divided the artistic and critical community between traditionalists (like Béla and his circle) and enthusiasts for the avant-garde (many of whom were Jewish). Similar developments were afoot in literature and music, with the poetry of Endre Ady and the challenging to-nalities of Béla Bartók. In a society like that of Budapest in 1914, in which culture (in an age when that word needed neither quotation marks nor qualification) held an almost sacred place in the lives of the educated classes, these controversies, and the increasing polar-ization of opinion around them, counted for a great deal.

Still, the material lives of the upper middle class and the gentry were comfortable and seemingly secure, with summers spent away from the oppressive heat of the city on the shores of Lake Balaton, the pleasant Adriatic coast (a day's travel by fast train), and in the Alps, with *Baedeker* in hand; or, for the wealthy, perhaps in Italy, or the smart resorts of the French Riviera and the Atlantic coast. These people, on the whole, encountered courtesy and deference wherever they went; like Béla, they could tip their way through life. Modern conveniences—the telephone, the electric tram, the motorcar, the espresso machine, aspirin—had become part of everyday life. Yet conversations turned, again and again, to seemingly insoluble politi-cal problems and threats, internal and external, to the established order. It was a society that managed to combine deep complacency with an uneasy sense that things could not go on as they were.

The one thing that practically nobody foresaw was what actually happened: a continent-wide "total" war lasting for four relentless years, by the end of which Austria-Hungary's human and material resources would be utterly exhausted, its institutions wrecked, and its very existence as an entity coming to an abrupt end.

The terrible toll of human lives and physical suffering imposed by the war of 1914–1918 on all of the combatant nations is its defining feature in our historical imagination. The losses suffered by Austria-Hungary are, nonetheless, still shocking. In just the first two weeks of fighting, the monarchy's casualties—killed, wounded, or captured—numbered 400,000;[4] by the end of 1914, over 850,000. The first three months of 1915 added another 800,000 to the casualty lists. More than 40 percent of these losses were from the Hungarian lands.[5] By the end of the war, Austro-Hungarian casualties were almost 7 million out of a population (in 1914) of 51 million. (For the sake of comparison, British casualties were 2.5 million out of a population of 46 million.)[6] An average of more than 4,500 Austro-Hungarian men in uniform were killed, wounded, or captured every single day of the war.

This recently discovered memoir covers a period of eight months, from the day that news of Austro-Hungary's declaration of war on Serbia reaches the little Adriatic resort where Béla is holidaying with friends to the day when—after brief military training, the hell of battle against the Russians on the Galician front, serious injury, and slow recuperation—he returns to Budapest in early April 1915 to report once more for duty. Vivid, acutely observant, and intensely personal, it offers a rare insight into a long-lost world and a largely

4. Norman Stone, *The Eastern Front 1914–1917* (London: Hodder & Stoughton, 1975), 91.
5. Cartledge, *The Will to Survive*, 312.
6. Niall Ferguson, *The Pity of War* (London: Allen Lane, 1998), 93, 295–96.

forgotten theater of the Great War, and into the engagingly skeptical and subtle mind of a man—and an artist—who is at once a
product of his age and privileged background, and a quietly sardonic
critic of the jingoism, folly, self-deception, and hypocrisy that he sees
all around him, as the country is first caught up in enthusiasm for
the war and then increasingly in denial of its realities.

At the heart of the narrative is the description of combat in the
sandy hills and forests of northern Galicia, deep inside what the his-
torian Timothy Snyder has called eastern Europe's "bloodlands"—
the scene of human slaughter on a vast scale in the twentieth century,
including the Nazi holocaust of European Jewry. (Oblivious, of
course, to what was to come, the author observes a remote Jewish
shtetl with a mixture of fascinated curiosity and the faint disdain
characteristic of his class and age.) There is no shortage of writing
about life at the front in the First World War (although firsthand
accounts of the Galician campaign of 1914 are rare);[7] nonetheless,
this record of the experience of battle stands out for its subjective
intensity, self-awareness, and richness of detail. It makes for terrify-
ing reading. It is no wonder that the writer emerged from the experience bearing, in addition to his physical wounds, psychological
damage (diagnosed, in the terminology of the day, as "traumatic
neurosis," but otherwise untreated) that haunts him and blocks his
artistic creativity during the months of his slow recuperation, and
left him inwardly scarred to the end of his long life.

The memoir is no less interesting for the picture it provides of the
culture and mores of the stylishly dressed but woefully ill-prepared
Austro-Hungarian army of 1914. (In this respect it complements Joseph Roth's great novel of military life, *The Radetzky March*.) Called
up as a junior reserve officer in the infantry, the young Béla observes,
with his distinctive laconic irony, the complacency and heartlessness
of the regular officer class, with its absurd insistence on punctilios of

---

7. John Keegan, *The First World War* (London: Random House UK Ltd, 1998),
174–75.

dress and decorative military ritual. About to go into the carnage at Rava Ruska, he is reprimanded for failing to present his sword on parade. ("This should really scare the Russians," he comments in a typically dry aside, as he straps on the useless ornament. "It's what makes a man fit for court," a Hungarian villager says later, awestruck at being allowed to touch the sacred object.) Troops are sent on long forced marches in full gear, rendering them useless for battle. Men ordered into withering artillery fire are forbidden to dig foxholes, as this "leads to cowardice and undermines discipline"; defying this homicidal instruction, they claw at the ground with discarded lids from tin cans and their bare hands as the barrage erupts around them.

But it is the account of what happens after his return from the front that is, from a psychological point of view, the most revealing and interesting part of the work. After a spell in the "crazies" ward of a military hospital, Béla becomes a lost soul, wandering the streets of his beloved Budapest in search of his past, a parody of the flaneur and young blade that he once was. He notes the changes that even a few weeks of a distant war have wrought on his city and its people: the trim little park trampled to mud, a porter yelling in the railway station, rowdiness at his favorite coffeehouse, and a sullen, silent struggle between those who have been conscripted and those who have not. As he revisits his old haunts, he feels the ties that bound him to the place dissolving and the city turning its back on him. There are intriguing echoes here of the classic early twentieth-century texts of the city as locus of alienation and memory. It is a quintessentially "modern" predicament—dislocation, the fruitless search to recover a past that was once whole and charged with meaning. It is the condition evoked in T. S. Eliot's *The Waste Land*, Hermann Hesse's *Steppenwolf*, and the paintings of Giorgio de Chirico.

In the final section of the book, the search for quietude and the wellspring of his creativity takes the author away from Budapest— first to a spell in the deep country, where memories of childhood and a still-undisturbed old order of parish life and village custom promise an escape of sorts, and where a reluctant encounter with rustic gastronomy (on the occasion of the slaughter of a prize pig) provides an episode of beautifully observed comic relief; and finally back to the sea, the Adriatic coast where he spent the last summer of peacetime, and where spring has already returned. Here, amid the beauty of his beloved warm south and the simple familial kindness of his hosts, he begins at last to find inner calm and to draw again. He is joined for a while by his friend and fellow artist Ervin, and together they explore the coastline and discuss what is happening to the world. Béla is filled with a sense of foreboding: "And all this is nothing compared with what still awaits us." But he is ready to face the uncertain future.

That future—in case the reader is curious to know how it turned out—was to be bound up in Hungary's troubled history after 1914.

Béla spent the rest of the war in uniform but away from the front. After a short period of training newly conscripted men, he was put in charge of a camp for Russian prisoners of war at Kissitke in western Hungary. The posting seems to have suited him well, and the beautifully worked wooden objects that he received from grateful prisoners, and treasured all his life, suggest that he encouraged handicrafts among his charges and treated them with humanity. In 1916 he returned to Budapest to work in the war ministry's information office as a designer; here he created, among other things, notable designs for posters for the war effort and to advertise exhibitions associated with it.[8] He was also responsible for designing the coronation ceremony of the hapless Karl in December 1916.

After the war, he returned to teaching at the Budapest School of Applied Arts, as he had done from 1909 to 1914; he became the principal in 1935 and an adviser to the education minister, for which he was honored. These were also years of recognition and success for him

---

8. Three of these are in the collection of the Imperial War Museum in London.

as a painter. His work (invariably realistic and "painterly" in style) won numerous prizes and was shown at the Barcelona International Exposition of 1929. He enjoyed particular success as a portraitist: sitters doubtless appreciated his traditionalism and technical skill in rendering what they would have regarded as a proper likeness.

Plain "Béla Moldován" until 1933, in that year he officially took his mother's family name as a prefix to his own. She was from an old titled family (Zombory de Tarczal) and had died when he was ten.

He was a lifelong conservative by temperament, a lover of old and well-worn things, and a determined disparager of modernist tendencies in art; but he disliked the increasingly rightward drift under the Horthy regime from the mid-1930s, and spurned an invitation to join the so-called Order of Gallantry (Vitézi Rend) established by the regime as elite guardians of the nationalist flame.[9] Following the German military occupation of Hungary in March 1944, at great personal risk, he sheltered a Jewish family from deportation and murder,[10] and he had nothing but contempt for the Hungarian Fascists, the Arrow Cross (Nyilasok), who came to power in October of that year. (He was characteristically bemused by the unannounced visit, shortly after the war, of a deputation from the local synagogue who insisted on blessing him as a "righteous Gentile.")

The establishment of a Moscow-sponsored Communist regime in Hungary after World War II was a personal as well as a national catastrophe. Béla was interrogated by the secret police, the dreaded ÁVO, at their headquarters at 60 Andrássy Avenue. In 1946, caught up in a purge of "right-wing elements" from public service in which some sixty thousand officials were removed from their posts, Béla was dismissed from the School of Applied Arts. Unable to sell his work and excluded from the state-approved artists' organizations

9. His motives for doing so may have been high-minded, although Cartledge observes in *The Will to Survive* that "the Order tended to be cold-shouldered by the nobility and gentry as social parvenus" (369).

10. Almost half a million Jews were deported from Hungary to Auschwitz between May and July 1944.

after the Communists tightened their grip on power from 1948, he withdrew into virtual seclusion, spending long periods alone in the little thatched summer house he had designed in the 1930s at Balatonfüred in western Hungary. There, he occupied himself with making paintings, watercolors, and etchings of the region's open landscapes and the shores of Lake Balaton, getting about on an ancient black bicycle. These are probably his finest body of work: Restrained, modest in scale, and filled with a quiet, calm luminosity, they express his love of the land. The writing of this memoir—part of an unfinished wider project—probably also dates from this period.

Béla Zombory-Moldován died at Balatonfüred on August 20, 1967.

My childhood memories of him are of his last years. He came to visit us in England when I was about six; an old man, but erect and dapper in a well-cut Prince of Wales check suit, leather gloves casually clasped in one hand, a homburg tilted just so above piercing eyes, and a neatly trimmed gray moustache. Even in those days, he seemed to belong to a distant, more graceful age. He spoke quietly and chose his words with care. He had the air of a man used to being respected.

I saw him again a year later. He and my grandmother were staying at Balatonfüred in the summer house, where the water had to be drawn by an ancient hand pump from an echoing well. He beckoned me into a stiflingly hot garden shed filled with the buzzing of wasps and the acrid smell of rotting pears. He sat in there, round-backed, on a rickety stool, palette in hand and dabbing at a hardboard panel clamped to a wobbly easel. I watched, not knowing what to say and anxious about the wasps. An oppressive hush lay everywhere. After a little while, he seemed to forget that I was there and to be immersed in thought. I slipped away as soon as I felt was polite. He only came into the house for meals and for his afternoon nap, when we all tiptoed around, even outside.

The last time I saw him was in the summer of 1967, when I was nine and he was dying. One evening, after the grown-ups had, one by one, visited him in his little bedroom, I was told that *nagyapu* wanted to see me. He lay on a narrow bed, unshaven, in an old flannel shirt. He could barely speak, but he gripped my hand, and I kissed his bristly cheek. The next morning I was told that he had been taken to the hospital, but everyone's eyes were very red, and I realized that was not true.

I later learned that he could be heard, during his last night, crying out in his sleep: "Get down! Get down! They're shooting from there too!"[11]

He had told no one about the writing to which he must have devoted so many solitary hours. The manuscript—on small sheets of cheap notepaper from various sources, individually trimmed to size with a paper knife and carefully numbered—was found by my grandmother, after his death, in a locked strongbox. She too kept it secret, passing it before she died to my uncle Pali in Germany. He subsequently gave it to my father, who showed it to me in 2012.

The yellowing sheets were covered to the edges with tight handwriting, as if paper were too dear to be wasted. At first, I could scarcely make out more than a few words of the Hungarian. By chance, as I leafed through the forbidding-looking pages, my eye was caught by what I soon realized was a quite remarkable firsthand account of battle. The more I read, the stronger became my impression that it was worth the effort, and that this material might be of more than family interest.

I tentatively began this translation in 2013, initially with the shortest chapter I could find, as an experiment. By then—with the patient assistance of my mother, who laboriously photocopied the manuscript and arranged for it to be transcribed—I was able to work from a typed version, which made the task much easier. What

---

11. *Feküdj! Feküdj! Onnan is lőnek!*

began to emerge, and the reaction of the few friends I showed it to, was sufficiently encouraging to induce me to undertake the entire project.

The manuscript is incomplete. It is clear, from slips of paper on which Béla evidently planned the outline of the project, that he intended something much larger, covering his life up to at least 1945 and possibly beyond. The existing manuscript runs out at 1915, in mid-chapter. (My grandmother may have withheld, or destroyed, some parts: It is notable that what survives ends just before she and Béla met.) There are several complete chapters about his childhood, school days, and youth, which I have left for another day.

With some trepidation, I have taken it upon myself to be not only my grandfather's translator but also his editor. I have performed the latter task acutely aware that he is not here to object, and conscious that the manuscript is now also a historical document, not lightly to be trifled with. At the same time, it seemed to me that a fragmentary work that gives out practically in mid-sentence is like an unfinished musical composition that ends in mid-bar: both need to be trimmed off, as it were, at a convenient point, even if this means leaving out some material that still bears the author's hand. Luckily, such a point presented itself in this case in a way that is (to my mind, at least) a satisfying close to the work, almost as if it had been intended that way, yet leaving a sense that the story is still only half told.

Perhaps more controversially, I have made a number of cuts, chiefly in the final chapter, of sometimes lengthy digressions and discursive polemics on topics of little or no relevance to the narrative, such as the relationship between photography and fine art, which would have tried the patience of even the most engaged reader. I have felt able to justify these interventions on the grounds that, had Béla ever offered up his work for publication, he would probably have received similar advice from his editor, which I like to think he would graciously have accepted.

Otherwise, I have changed as little as possible. A very long last chapter has been divided into three, and I have supplied titles to these. The book's title, which I have also supplied, is borrowed from the text. The epilogue is taken from the fragmentary material pruned from the end. Paragraph breaks and ellipses have been introduced where I felt that clarity and sense required them. In a few instances I have corrected what appear to be slips, the more significant of which I have recorded in the notes to the text.

My thanks are due to the people whose assistance made my task a great deal easier. Dr. Erika Östör was instrumental in arranging for the manuscript's transcription and answered numerous queries. Ilona Csiszér and Erika Kaltenecker performed miracles in deciphering the text. Péter Geszti generously gave me his father's copy of László Országh's fine Hungarian-English dictionary of 1953. Anita Salamon of the Budapest School of Applied Arts kindly provided biographical information. Between them, Klaudia Trzcielinska and Siward Atkins cracked a Slavic puzzle. Stephen Unwin commented perceptively on an early draft of the translation and made valuable suggestions for the introduction. George Poulos, Judith Brown, Charles Darwent, and Tom Grant provided encouragement when it was most needed. I am especially grateful to Professor István Deák for the kind interest he showed in the project and for saving me from falling into historical error at several points in the introduction. (Errors that remain are entirely of my own making.) Above all, the tireless help of my mother and father, who patiently answered my innumerable questions—lexical, cultural, biographical, and geographical—made this translation possible, and I gratefully dedicate it to them.

—PETER ZOMBORY-MOLDOVAN
London, May 2014

THE BURNING OF THE WORLD

1. NOVI

I HAD SLEPT badly. The previous day, the usual group of us had gone on an outing to Bribir.[1] Knoll, who was a county magistrate, had planned the itinerary. A stocky, energetic little man, he had even prepared a talk extolling the historic friendship between the Hungarians and the Croats, noting the castle's former associations with Hungary. Judge Kriegl's two daughters were lively young women, and easy company. Antal Hajnal, from the Franklin publishing house, was there; his factotum, Jankoviusz, flirted outrageously with one of the Kriegl girls. There was much eating and drinking of *vino nero*, and almost childlike high spirits. The fun had continued afterwards back at the pension, where we went on to beer. Having paid too little regard to what they say about mixing grape and grain, I was woken by nausea more than once during the night. There were no more serious ill effects, but I rose in the morning feeling like a somnambulist.

I decided to go for an early solitary swim. I managed to slip out unnoticed, and headed for the spit of land which separated the harbor from the open sea. On the far side stretched the sandy beach and the bathing station. When I reached the highest point on the spit, I slackened my pace and took in the mirror-flat water stretching to infinity. It was sleeping calmly now, though it was capable of such cruelty; even so, I loved it. I could never have enough of this beauty.

Unusual to have it all to myself. But a male figure was coming up towards me from the beach, in some haste. The bathing attendant.

I had no inkling that the course of my life would be decided in the next few minutes.

"Good morning." He stopped. "Well, I say goodbye now." He struggled a little with the Hungarian.

"Why? You're not leaving, are you?"

"Leaving? I must go in the army. There is going to be war."

"What are you talking about?" Aghast, I stared at him.

"Please. The notice is there on the wall of the bathing station." As if in a trance, I grasped the hand he was holding out to me; mechanically, I thanked him for his services and gave him a five-korona piece.

Then I raced to the bathing station. It was all shut up, and on its wall was a notice which listed call-up dates by year of birth. I was to report for service at Veszprém—*Veszprém*!—with the Thirty-First Regiment of the Royal Hungarian Army by the fourth of August.[2] I stared at the poster as if I had just suffered a stroke, reading it over and over, until I realized that I was just looking at the words rather than taking in the meaning.

Only one word mattered: war.

There had been no war in Hungary for almost seventy years. When my grandfather spoke of 1848,[3] we would listen with bored half smiles: it was all so alien to us, so far removed from us. This was the twentieth century! Europe at equilibrium in the era of enlightenment and democratic humanism. It seemed impossible that a dispute should be decided by fighting. This couldn't be true! They were going to shoot at me, or stab me, or I was going to shoot at a complete stranger with whom I had no quarrel, whom I didn't even know, who would be mourned just as I would be, into whom I would jab a bayonet fixed to a six-kilo rifle and feel the cracking and juddering as it tore his chest open. "A soldier dies, that others may live." Fine words! But I am twenty-nine, at the start of my career, filled with plans and the urge to create, with some early success. I want to work! I was born to create, and I loathe destruction of any kind.

My legs carried me on, as if automatically, along the familiar path. I had reached the bay. I stood transfixed by the sight of a sailing boat, gazing at its yard. What a pretty gallows it would make! One could hang a good half-dozen men from that boom.

I didn't want to be among people. I turned off the shore towards the right, onto the coastal footpath they call the *lungomare*. There I found a stone bench. It must have been put up in someone's memory: a medallion in the center was carved with a profile in relief. Yesterday, I might have taken a look at it; today, it no longer interested me.

Before me, the calm sea, the susurration of wavelets washing onto the sandy shore. The monster was asleep now. It cared nothing about what happened to the various beings that lived ashore. Sometimes it became enraged, and shook off the man-fleas that had dared to venture onto its back; after that, it took no further interest in them.

A scorpion made its way along the edge of the path. I might have trodden it underfoot yesterday. Today, I couldn't be bothered. I watched it disinterestedly. Then it crawled into a gap in the rock.

I ought to sort out my affairs. Sebők had sent me an express letter yesterday with a subject for a drawing for the magazine,[4] and I had done nothing about it yet. I should be sending it off today. Never mind. They wouldn't want any illustrations this week. Anyway, I ought to visit the editorial office. Better to telephone. I could do without the farewells and the handshaking. But having to say goodbye to my parents! And relations, and friends. I'd rather join up in secret.

Light footsteps on the path's gravel. Ervin Voit[5] sat down beside me. A pause; then his fine, quiet voice. "I've been looking all over for you. We wondered what had become of you."

I gave him a sideways look and spread my hands. We sat silently a good while, watching the glittering sky and listening to the demented rasping of the cicadas. Everything as it was yesterday. The death of one man, of a hundred, of a million, is nothing to nature's hurdy-gurdy. Everything goes on as before. Perhaps it is only man that makes such a fuss about dying.

"We were expecting you at lunch. That's why I came to find you." We set off.

"Have you been called up as well?"

"I'm going home tomorrow, and then on from there."

The dining room had changed. All the usual convivial noise,

larking about, and tittering had ceased. The guests had gathered at separate tables according to their nationalities. Groups which had previously spread themselves around now clustered together. Sereghy and his wife had come over to join us. Czechs, Serbs, Croats, Germans—all sat apart. People leaned in together over the tables and discussed events with animated gestures and low voices.

As we entered, I was met with searching looks from the members of our group. Ervin responded with quiet nods. Kriegl broke the silence.

"Oh well, it's obvious who the best-dressed young man among us is." His forced joviality was meant to relieve the strained atmosphere. I put on a smile and sat down.

"This isn't going to be too serious. A little punitive operation in Serbia, and we'll be done in a jiffy."

"Shh!" whispered Sereghy, raising his forefinger and turning his eyes meaningfully towards the Serbs' table.

Kriegl blushed, hunching his shoulders and putting a finger across his lips.

The "Czech Uncle"—a Czech university teacher from whom Ervin and I had taken a few lessons in Czech, which had made him treat us with great friendliness—was now stiffly formal and sat solemnly at the Czechs' table.

Everyone spoke in their mother tongue, as if encyphering what they had to say.

I said that I would be leaving for home tomorrow.

"What's the hurry? You don't have to report until the fourth."

"Stay another couple of days."

"I can't." I shook my head. "There are things I've got to sort out, and I need to write a will." I was unsure whether I was joking.

"I hope you leave one of your pictures to me."

"No one's going to inherit my pictures. I'm having them burnt." Nobody laughed.

Lunch went on dispiritedly, amid naïve speculation about how the war would go, expressions of confidence, and feigned cheerfulness. The division into separate nationalities and races became absolute. A Hungarian schoolmistress joined our table. She had not spoken to us before.

"What's going to happen now? I'm not staying any longer. I can't wait to get home."

Mrs. Kriegl turned to her husband. "Shouldn't we be going as well?" Kriegl argued in favor of staying, but more out of affected bravery than conviction.

Everyone felt that this was no longer the Novi[6] in which we could feel as much at home, and as safe, as if we were in Hungary itself. It had already become a foreign Novi. The hills, the villages, the houses, the sea, the people—everything was foreign. We parted in oppressive silence.

During the afternoon, I sought solitude and walked the familiar paths, the cliffs along the shore, and the little sandy inlets where, in a rough sea, the waves can be eight or ten meters high. I sent a telegram home and another to the Franklin.

We met again at dinner. There was something almost ostentatious now about the separation of nationalities. The Slavs huddled together. The Germans looked the least concerned: a huge country with a fearsome army.

The subject of my departure came up.

"Are you really going? It seems a shame to rush, when you could spend another four days here."

"I know you're being sincere. We've had such lovely times together; and it would feel better now if more of us stayed. But I must go, if only because of my parents. I'm their only child, and they'll be worried about me. Besides, there's so much I need to sort out. So I'm going to say thank you to everyone now for their kindness and friendship. These will be unforgettable memories that I take with me."

I stood, bowed, and went up to my room.

Leaning on the sill of an open window, I gazed out at the darkly glinting sea and the sparkle of the stars in their billions. The deep stillness was broken by the occasional distant sound or song. From the dining room down below, there usually rose up a continuous buzz of commotion, brightened now and then by women's laughter;

now that, too, was quiet, with only the occasional sound or fragment of conversation filtering out at the opening of a door. The silence was broken by approaching sounds of loud singing and raucous shouts. Drunken sailors. Sharp knocks echoed off the walls in the street outside. The most drunken among them launched into a fresh rendition of "Magyarszki Reporting."[7] Laughter as the others tried to quieten him down. Then more yelling, but now from the next street.

There we are. Fraternal affection between the nations of the Monarchy.

I closed the window and lay down on the bed in my clothes. It would be good to read something. I found Sebők's and Elek Benedek's[8] notes on the topics for illustration in the weekly issues. Before coming, I had done two weeks' worth of drawings, and since then I received instructions every Monday by express post and sent the drawings back, also express, on Wednesdays. Sometimes, with everything going on here, I forgot the details of a particular character from one issue to the next. On one occasion, Benedek had written, rather crossly, that I kept altering his hero: "Karcsi gets shorter by the issue, looks different and changes his hairstyle. He can now barely see over the top of the table." Deeply embarrassed, I sent him an apologetic letter and started to make Karcsi grow by stages. It was all right in the end. Dear, kind old Elek Benedek, with his lovely stories. Would I ever see him again? And Zsigmond Sebők, always calm and softly spoken, always a gentleman. He lived in Damjanich Street, where he liked best of all to decamp to the bathroom to write his *Dörmögő Dömötör* bear stories for the magazine. I would never forget how good he had been to me.

I picked up an illustrated brochure and leafed through it as I lay on my back. Cherso, Veglia, Arbe, Lussino[9]... so many beautiful places, such romance ... I should get undressed and into bed. Just a little longer among these memories ...

I was startled awake by a soft knocking on the door. I had fallen asleep in my clothes. Ervin opened the door quietly.

"You're dressed already?" I could barely see him through my swollen eyelids.

"I seem to have nodded off. What time is it?"

"I think you need to be going soon. It's morning. I came to see you off."

I undressed quickly, and a cold-water wash to the waist sorted me out. I must have been a comical sight as I dried myself off: I looked as if I were wearing a white vest, those portions of me which had not been covered by my bathing costume having been tanned to a chestnut brown. This would be my souvenir. The sight of this color would recall my memories.

I grabbed my things together and we set off at a brisk pace on what was quite a long walk. We could already see, in the distance, the black Ungaro-Croata line steamer as it approached the jetty.

"Look, I had a chance to think things over last night. Don't misunderstand me. Forget my work, and my parents' anxiety. Not everyone has to die in a war, I know that. The stupid bullet, on the other hand, doesn't know; but never mind that now. That's not what I'm talking about. I just can't describe—I can't even name—the shapeless, ungraspable, amorphous mass that I have to carry. Sometimes it weighs so heavily on me that I'm ready to collapse under it. Out of this formless mass, now and then, certain signs flash out: How long will this last? Or: Once it's over, what happens then? Or: How on earth is Hungary going to get out of this? And so on, and on. Each question branches out into more and more questions, and once you start, you get nowhere. One thing I've noticed, though, is that the more narrow-minded a person is, the more easily he finds a way through this maze. He'll declare confidently, for instance: We'll soon teach the Serbs their lesson, and that'll be that. Afterwards, a victorious Hungary will prosper, increasing its influence over the Balkans. Hungary will win because it has to: it's obvious. Lucky people. It doesn't matter to them if events prove them wrong, because they immediately find another, equally certain, solution.

"This war may just be the first act of a global tragedy. It's as if someone were struggling against an angry sea, while behind his back towers an immense wall of ice, ready to collapse onto him at any moment. This is the socialist revolution which will, one day, fall with full force on nations weakened by war. The war could be the least of our problems. Socialism has been agitating and organizing for the past hundred years. It's just waiting for the opportunity to take power. Maybe it would be better if it did: one of its basic principles is to put an end to wars of conquest. Maybe it'll be they who stop this war, if political theory and practice coincide for once.

"I remember one of our walks with Jaschik, beyond the city park, towards the Rákosi marshaling yards, where we waited to see the Vienna fast train, the new Class In engine chattering and thundering as it charged on towards Pest. It was gigantic, an awe-inspiring sight that seized the imagination. On the way back, we talked about political questions, and the endless demonstrations. One thing was certain: the twentieth century would be the century of the Jews, and of revolutions.

"It's a curious phenomenon that Jews, who are born capitalists, are the ones rousing the workers against capital. Or is it this: they invented artistic revolution, and they proclaim it from the rooftops. They put no value on tradition in the ceaseless pursuit of the new. The twentieth century opened with the *Sezession* and the pace keeps quickening. We're at 'The Eight'[10] now. We're living in times that feel as if we were hopping about on top of an overheating boiler, waiting for the explosion.

"Maybe all this is just in my imagination. Maybe the optimists are going to be proved right. But I really can't see a way out of this. This war seems to me to be like first shudder of cold down a man's spine. The real sickness is yet to come.

"Well, the boat's here. I need to get on board. There's no point in all this talk and speculation. Even if I do get back, we'll all be living different lives. It's goodbye to the good old days."

We embraced in silence.

"Heaven bless you all."

Lips trembling, Ervin tried to speak; but only a tear rolled down his cheek.

I practically ran up the gangplank. I did not look back.

The antiquated black steamer was crammed; even the mast and

cranes were festooned with drafted men, half of them drunk. Waves were hitting the vessel's side, and as it left the harbor and reached the open sea, it began to pitch about quite seriously. I squirmed myself into a tiny space on the landward side, from where, propped on my suitcase, I watched the hazy shore.

I felt a little easier. I had said goodbye to my friends and to my former life at the same time. I had broken with the past, and now I occupied myself with the future. I had to consider even the smallest detail. It ought to be possible to anticipate whatever circumstances lay ahead. I had no experience to fall back on. Anything I had heard of war had fallen on deaf ears; an anachronism, it had held no meaning for me. No one in my family since my grandfather had been in a war. They knew even less about it than I did, and had no experience on which I might draw. Until it confronted us, everyone had regarded war as an absurdity. Now it was a reality. If it was any consolation, the enemy must be having the same problem. Except that they had learned to handle firearms up there in the mountains of Serbia. We might pay a price for the blithe and vacuous existence we had led here.

As we came to the lesser stops on the route, instead of the ship docking, smaller boats came out to meet us. It was a wonder that the drunks on them all managed to stay aboard. Sometimes these boats smacked into the ship's side; sometimes they danced on the tops of waves above the gunwale. Shrieking, swearing, laughing, the passengers just kept on coming. Where would they all go? The situation was starting to look alarming. The drunks couldn't care less: they just roared away at the tops of their cracked voices. I tried to judge how far we were from shore, and wondered if I would be able to swim it. Next stop, Crikvenica. More passengers. The captain was shouting. By the time we got to Porto Re,[11] he allowed no one else to board. I knew these places well and had spent happy days in all of them; perhaps it was fortunate that, in the circumstances, I had no time for reminiscence. I will never know how we made it all the way to Fiume[12] and managed to dock. As for disembarkation: a crazed mob. I stood back to let the crowd surge past me.

A train was waiting to depart at the railway station, puffing impatiently. A great mass of people here as well, fed by the crowds from other boats. I had to struggle to get a place. At last, the huge engine got under way, its four cylinders driving twelve wheels. A glimpse of the glorious panoramic view down to Buccari; then the majestic cliffs and bare landscapes of the Karst and the massive walls of stone facing the Bora.[13] From the pass at Lič, more than a thousand meters up, a farewell glimpse of the distant view disappearing behind the opal mist—and the sea was gone.

From here, we raced downhill all the way to Zagreb. I managed to get a seat by an open window. The reverberations of the train as it thundered and clattered among cliffs, though forests and tunnels, drowned out the racket from the passengers behind me. None of them was interested in the landscapes we were passing through. They shouted each other down as they argued over events.

This was how I made the journey home, to face a changed world.

2. BUDAPEST AT WAR

TIME WAS when this line thrilled me: Budapest—Fiume![1] I could recite the stops on the express service off by heart. Now I sat quietly in a corner. The magic had evaporated. Sunk into myself, I tried to put what needed to be done into some logical order. There was no one to turn to for advice; I would have to work this out for myself. It had been drummed into me during military service[2] that a good soldier carries out his orders without thinking, like a machine. There are others to do the thinking for him. That was all very well, but a man who didn't think for himself was doomed. The color of a piece of clothing, the glint of a weapon, an ill-chosen bit of cover, an unfortunate sudden nervous movement—who knows, any trivial little thing could mean the difference between life and death. Orders are orders: fine. But secretly I felt that my duty to myself was paramount. Indeed, without that, there would soon be no one left to order about. This now seemed so obvious that it amazed me that, during my military service as a private, the very thought of it had been forbidden. Even now, I must keep these thoughts to myself and breathe not a word of them, or the fervent crowd would spit on me as a coward.

"Our boys!"

"They'll show 'em!"

"Hungarian valor!"

As such phrases flew about, the loudest of my fellow passengers were the old and the children. Rowdily, and for the second time now, there came from the next compartment the words of the new war song:[3]

Just you wait,
Just you wait,
Serbia, you dog!

The voices of the old and the young; voices of women, too. *Toréador,
l'amour t'attend!*[4]

———

The train charged on. The stations: Rétszilas ... Simontornya ... All
these names, once so redolent of charm, rang hollow now. We were
approaching Budapest. There was growing bustle on the train. I
wished they weren't waiting for me at the station. The best thing
would be to get off at Kelenföld: there would definitely be nobody
waiting there, and I'd have time, while I jolted my way home in a
cab, to put on a cheerful and enthusiastic face. So I did.

It took me more than half an hour to get home, near the Eastern
Station. I rang the doorbell and waited for my mother[5] to come to
the door. The main thing was to show a confident gaiety. Excellent
holiday! Mentally and physically refreshed, ready for anything! The
call-up? Got to do my bit! Anything to stop her from getting a word
in. It was getting late; I'd have to go to bed soon; anyway, I was tired
out, and had a mountain of things to do tomorrow. And the day after, I would already be on my way to Veszprém.

My mother opened the door. She had just got back from the station, where she had been waiting for me.

"We must have missed each other in the crowd. What do you
think of my suntan? Everyone's been admiring it. I hope there's
something nice for dinner, mother dear. I had hardly anything to eat
on the whole journey."

"Everyone's been asking after you. Zsigmond Sebők, the school,
painters. E—— H—— was here, she left a big bouquet for you, there
it is on the table. Poor girl! Why don't you like her? You'll be the
death of her."

"Don't, please. You're making me feel bad."

My father at my back the whole time. "I'd really like to talk to you."

"Tomorrow. I'm awfully tired right now."

"Uncle Béla has sent you an express letter. Here you are."

"I'll read it in bed. Good night."

The familiar bed, the bedside cabinet with its thoughtful little lace coverlet, my books, my little reading lamp... Dear Uncle Béla! His clerically soothing, pure-hearted lines penned in his copper-plate hand: he asks for God's blessing on me and he will pray for me. My tears ran into the pillowcase. From the street outside, I heard the drunken bellowing of the "unfit for service":

Get that nasty thing out,
Pull it out of there!
Never mind, just leave it in,
It's fine there, I don't care![6]

Next day, my mother was up early; I could hear her carefully open-ing and closing drawers in the next bedroom. Later on, she crept up to my door and slowly turned the handle, so that it creaked (which it never did when one turned it quickly). "He's still sleeping," she whispered back, articulating the words slowly. Afterwards, the quiet creaking of doors, then the sound of my father descending the stairs, audible through the wall of my room. I dragged myself slowly to my feet, tidied myself up, and flung open the door with a loud "good morning." I found myself face to face with my mother, her reddish eyes smiling at me, her look searching. I could see that she, too, had put on a mask.

I held her arm; she placed her free hand over mine, and led me to the dining table, on which a huge breakfast had been lovingly laid out. I gabbled on about how much I had to do and how many places I had to go today, all the things I had to think of, all the packing I needed to do. Would she put some underwear together for me? I couldn't take much, this wasn't a holiday I'd be going on where everyone showed off their wardrobes. Who'd be doing my laundry? I didn't know; this wasn't something that was covered in the Service Regulations. I might even be like the outlaw in Papa's lovely old song:

Nor roof, nor barn, nor herd is mine
But bed and pillow both of stone
For company I have the night
And rain to wash my cover white.

I even sang it; but my voice was hoarse and uncertain. My mother inclined her head and was solemn. Right, time I got going.

The street was full of hurrying people. I walked down Dohány Street; my studio was in the Lajos Ernst building at the corner of Miksa Street. With the studio was a sitting room, hall, bathroom and kitchen, but I used only the studio. My neighbors were Valér Ferenczy,[7] Baroness Ernesta Splényi,[8] and Móricz Sándor.[9] I didn't want to see any of them. They didn't even need to know that I had been called up. I sat down at the drawing table, where I had done so many illustrations for *Dörmögő Dömötör* and all kinds of other things. The familiar little indentations in the pine table top, the drawing-pin marks, the spatters of Indian ink. All of them friends. The witnesses and assistants to my work. And my unfinished pictures. The blank canvases and stretchers in the sitting room, the easel inherited from Ödön Tull,[10] the palettes and the brushes, the folding screens, the draperies. All quietly there, all waiting for me. Faithful friends.

I slipped quietly downstairs. On the Ring Boulevard,[11] the ground-floor windows of a daily paper's offices in the New York building displayed enormous hand-lettered sheets of paper announcing the latest news, updated hourly.[12] A huge crowd seethed in front of it. Noisy uproar, argument, and grandiloquence. Street-urchins running in every direction. "Latest!" From further off, the sound of singing. Enlisted men in military caps pinned all over with flowers. Hurrah! Hurrah! People throwing flowers at them. They stepped out proudly, enjoying the approbation. Along the teeming boulevard to Andrássy Avenue. I wanted to do some shopping, but for what? What does a spoiled young habitué of Pest's coffeehouses, bars, and parties need when he's going off to war? Who would know? Whom should I ask? I don't think anyone knows. People probably buy up all kinds of nonsense, which they then throw away. That, at any rate, I would avoid. Actually, I didn't need to buy anything other than a decent pair of waterproof boots and some warm socks and underwear, which I did. (The boots soaked through the first time they got wet; the underwear stood me in good stead, although I had to wear it for three weeks.) They tried to flog me a pair of jodhpurs as well, but I wasn't falling for that.

I felt tired. So much the better. Emotive memories were starting to have less of an effect on me. Even so, I ambled along Kazinczy Street and gazed up at the window of my old studio. Lajos Markó![13] Jenő Fülöp![14] Where are you? Then up Andrássy Avenue, to see the Academy one last time.[15]

I turned into Izabella Street for a farewell glance at the third studio window from the left, then I stroked the pillar at the entrance. At the corner of Szív Street, I peered cautiously through the window of the Fészek coffeehouse;[16] it was difficult, with the daylight, to identify the figures sitting and moving about in the dim interior. I could only make out as shadowy forms the silhouettes of the figures seated with their espressos around the usual table. I slipped in just behind a man who was going in, so as not be recognized. There didn't seem to be many there. Teplánszky[17] was in his customary place, holding forth. I felt a little ashamed to be slinking about, but I didn't feel up to any of the inevitable chitchat. I trudged on past where the old Kairó coffeehouse used to be: our old haunt, with all its fond memories, and the frescoes by Zsigmond Vajda[18] I had gazed at so many times.

Dog tired, I returned home for lunch. My father was already there, waiting for me. How wonderful just to wander around until one is exhausted! My nerves felt weary; I was starting to accept things as they were, and to treat the situation as a new experience.

Slowly, I put aside the mask I had been wearing, and noticed the easing of tension in my parents' faces as well. We discussed the situation, and how things were likely to develop, with a kind of cool equanimity. My father had brought reassuring (too reassuring) news from the office: apparently, the Royal Hungarian Army could not be deployed beyond the borders.

"Write as soon as you get there. Write every day. The post office has issued new field postcards; they give them out free. We want to know where you are every single day. That will be what we live for."

I promised to do everything they asked. Then I started to pack. I picked up objects that were familiar to me, to which I had grown accustomed, but I scarcely looked at them now. I had had enough of goodbyes. But as I lay in my bed, the terror that this might be my last night of home flooded over me.

The next day, I rose so that we would have no more than a half hour together before I had to leave.

"Please, Papa. Don't come to see me off."

My father's face was pale, as if he had barely slept all night. His moustache tilted slightly, then he gave a silent nod. My mother flung herself onto the bed, her whole body shaking as she sobbed mutely. Quickly, I turned away and pulled the door quietly shut behind me.

3. VESZPRÉM

I HAD NEVER been to Veszprém.[1] Szily Pongrácz's family used to talk about it because her uncle, Bishop Ranolder, used to have his palace there. He had crowned the Empress Elisabeth queen of Hungary in 1867,[2] as a consequence of which the court had heaped favors upon him. They inherited a splendid summer palace in Csopak from him, from the proceeds of which they purchased an estate in nearby Paloznak. This was all that I knew about Veszprém and about Lake Balaton, which—as a lover of the sea—I held in low esteem, regarding it as a malodorous puddle.

Veszprém was where I had to report for duty. My train took four hours to rattle its way there at an average of thirty kilometers an hour. The journey afforded me the opportunity to observe, along one curve in the line, that our engine resembled those that Ödön Tull used to draw for *Dörmögő Dömötör*. (After I took over from him, Dörmögő tore along with a Class In locomotive.) The train was half empty, which puzzled me. I was traveling in uniform, with a travel warrant, which had a magical effect, and I received looks of respect befitting a future hero.

At the conductor's helpful suggestion, I got off at the smaller station, as that was where I would find the corps and headquarters of the Thirty-First Regiment of the Royal Hungarian Army. I presented myself with purposeful vigor, and was received in a similar but friendly manner by an adjutant first lieutenant. I was given the address of my lodgings and five hundred korona—not in gold coin, but in banknotes and silver.[3] During the formalities, the lieutenant addressed me as "Ensign," but after that, he adopted a friendly tone and addressed me informally.

"You could have taken your time, you know. You have until the fourth to sign in."

"Well, better early than too late, I thought."

"True. Anyway, you won't be needed until the fourth. Have a look round, relax a bit; once the fun starts, you won't have much time to yourself. The main thing is to buy yourself a decent revolver from a hardware store."

I found someone to carry my things. I had been billeted to a very handsome and elegant house. I believe the owner was a director of a bank. They greeted me warmly and asked me a lot of questions. In conversation they were sanguine about the war and confident of its likely outcome. I had the impression that this enthusiastic note had been struck for my benefit; naturally, I had to adopt it myself—indeed, to surpass it. My suspicion was that, amongst themselves, they took a rather different view.

I took myself off to the main restaurant for dinner. Its fine terrace looked out over a park, on the far side of which was a convent school and church. The new theater, by Medgyaszay,[4] was to the right; its decoration, in the manner of Ödön Lechner,[5] took its inspiration from Hungarian folk embroidery. Evening fell as I dined, and a feeling of well-being began to come over me. I felt very much alone, though: my usual companions a hundred miles away, my friends and associates, and all the objects of my interests, unattainably remote. I had not yet made any new acquaintances, and if I did, what would we talk about? At best, the war.

I sauntered slowly home. A side entrance in the formally laid out garden and some steps led up to my room. The bed had been made nicely and there were fresh flowers on the table. I undressed at leisure, swallowed a glass of the *pálinka*,[6] and stretched myself out on the unfamiliar but perfectly comfortable new chaise longue. After a few moments I could hear, from beneath the open window, a shuffling noise and muffled laughter. I sprang to the window to see, running off from the shrubbery below, the two giggling housemaids. The young hero had been spied upon *en déshabillé*! A little put out, I lay down again; then smiled as I considered the opportunity for an escapade, though I was in no mood for it. I went on thinking for a good while about the life I had left behind, and found it hard to get to sleep, waking up at every unfamiliar little sound.

I awoke the next day to rather more hustle and bustle. Crowds of men arriving to sign on started to flood in. The regimental cadre was forming three operational regiments: a field regiment, a march regiment, and a territorial regiment. Twelve thousand men in all. That was more than the entire population of Veszprém. Where would they all go? What about hygiene arrangements? Let others worry about that. I had done well, at any rate, to turn up early, as I had got excellent lodgings.

I went off shopping and wandered through the town's maze of hilly streets. There were a few interesting old houses, picturesque ruins and old watermills, the splendid Séd valley, the Betekints inn and the deep, dark shade under its great trees, cliffs; a wealth of painterly subjects. Even the old people greeted me, and children followed me at a distance. But all of this—like all wonders—barely lasted three days; indeed, it ebbed by the hour in proportion to the torrent of men streaming into the town.

I was assigned to the march regiment: fourth battalion, fourth company. Our company commander was Captain József Kovács. Under him, four junior officers—Kovács, Földes, Osztermann, and me—as the platoon leaders. I was the most junior amongst them in rank, but third in age. The other three had done their year's military service straight after secondary school, and so had overtaken me in rank. We soon got to know one another and I felt we would become good "mates." The captain quizzed each of us and I told him what I did. I could see that he liked the look of me, and he confided that he was not really an infantryman, but a teacher of descriptive geometry and topography at a military academy.

Work began on the fourth of August. We took over our platoons and immediately started practicing drill, over and over. The drill in-structor had been a guard sergeant at the Illava prison.[7] He treated the poor old squaddies accordingly.

Of the four of us, only Földes had served in the Royal Hungarian Army; the rest of us didn't know the Hungarian commands.[8] By great good fortune, Földes owned a copy of the Service Regulations. We would lie in a circle on the parade-ground turf—at some risk, since the parade ground also served as pasture for some uncouth geese—and take turns swotting up the Regulations, whilst listening to the tramp of the units as they were drilled, and the drill instruc-tor's hoarse bellowing and cursing.

"Someone should have a word with Csambalik and tell him not to yell like that."

"Let him yell. If he didn't do it, we'd have to." This was Kovács, who had seniority in rank.

"All right. I'll grant you it has some intimidatory psychological effect, but most of these are family men of about thirty, thinking to themselves that just because they're going to die for their country, there's no need to treat them like animals."

"Incorrigible idealist!"

"He's yelling like that because the drill keeps going wrong. But it keeps going wrong because he can't keep time properly, and so their movements are affected by arrhythmia."

"Go on, tell him!"

"You outrank us, it's your job to educate him."

"If the bloody man wants to yell, he'll yell. This lot aren't exactly the Knights of Malta yet.[9] Come on, back to the Regulations."

If it was good enough for them, it would be good enough for me. It was something else to get used to. Anyway, I had started, the first night I was there, while I was still alone, to realize that all sorts of fancy ideas had to be put aside and forgotten about. I was being hit by a landslide of events and, since I couldn't run away from it, I had better work out how to dodge about well enough to avoid being flat-tened by it. One could get used to catastrophe, too; in fact, one had to get used to it. The past was gone. If I had the time for it, and if I was safe, I might daydream about it. But there was no point to it now. I had to summon all my imagination to grasp the situation and the circumstances that awaited me, and somehow to ensure my survival. Besides, now that Veszprém had more soldiers than inhabitants, there was a feeling of safety in numbers, and a sense of inner calm was starting to overtake me. From this enormous mass of men—even with so many long faces among them—surely some potent force would arise.

Solamen miseris socios habuisse doloris.[10] Just about every officer in the Army seemed to be camped out in the town's main coffeehouse every evening, to the accompaniment of champagne and a gypsy band. For want of anything better to do, I joined them. An opera bass, Pogány,[11] and a tenor, Diskay,[12] sang this and that, and we indulged in a certain amount of revelry. Making our way home late at night, we certainly disturbed the quiet of the streets. Pogány's rich voice rang out down the echoing lanes. Diskay kept wrapping his throat in scarves and was anxious to save his voice. If I got to my lodgings to lie down, I shut my eyes fitfully, occasionally hearing the giggling of the housemaids; but I was tired out, and tried my best to get some sleep.

I rose at five in the morning and had breakfast at the coffeehouse. Parade was at seven. Our march to the parade ground took us up the steep road past my lodgings. I signaled to the drummer, Dráfi, who beat time splendidly. The two housemaids came running out of the gate. For the fun of it, I gave the order: "Eyes right!" The girls' eyes shone with delight. If I was asked to explain myself over this, I would say that it was for practice. But I kept an absolutely straight face, and got away with it.

———

One day, as I was making my way to lunch, someone waved to me from a dilapidated cab. My father! Since I had left, he said, he had not slept a wink. Why had he come? He had wanted to see me one last time.

No more hardened resignation now: my wounds had been

reopened. He could see that I was upset, and there were tears in his eyes as he set off back to Budapest.

I didn't go to my usual place to dine that evening, or to the coffeehouse. I wandered about in the valley of the Séd, among the old watermills, until late in the evening. I was in very low spirits. The Betekints inn was still lit, and I ate some scrambled eggs.

I was still affected the next day, and the knowledge that my discomposure had caused my father pain weighed on my conscience.

————

The ceremonial giving of the oath of service was to take place the following Sunday on the square in front of the minster church, and on the Monday we would begin the seventy-five kilometer march to Keszthely.[13]

The mass was celebrated by the bishop, with a full supporting cast. It has to be said that the entire regiment of four thousand men reciting the words of the oath together created a very solemn effect. I made a bit of a mess of things as we paraded away from the square in double ranks, when I couldn't think of the Hungarian command for *Reien fällt ab*; on the spur of the moment, I translated this as "fall out in rows," whereupon the members of the platoon headed off in a variety of directions. The battalion commander, Captain Gyenes, was ready to have me trampled underfoot. At least it gave my fellow officers something to snigger about.

That night we bade farewell to Veszprém in style. Even more champagne than usual got put away, and I had a poor night's sleep. Early the next morning I wrote a few words of thanks to my kind and courteous hosts. I also said goodbye to the housemaids, pressing ten korona into the hands of each of them. One of them burst into tears, wiping her eyes and nose on her apron.

4. THE MARCH

ANOTHER farewell. A ceremonial parade accompanied by resounding marches from the band, interspersed alternately by trumpets and drums to keep time. Crowds had turned out to shower us with flowers. Beside me marched little Dráfi, the gypsy, who pattered away on his drum. I told him to stop it, but it was oddly catching. Just what I needed!

This idiotic seventy-five kilometer march had been ordered by the regimental commander, former staff officer Bél Sérsits, who was from Kissár. By the time we reached our destination, half the regiment had been rendered unfit for action from damage to their feet and general exhaustion.

As we left town, the band stood aside, and with them the flock of children and young people who had accompanied us the whole way. As we passed, they pressed into our hands the flowers they had brought with them. A little old lady wiped her eyes and made the sign of the cross at us. The band played the Radetzky March over and over, without a pause, until the entire column had passed.

Silence fell; then the drums struck up to keep step. A kind of numbness descended over the column, deadening the sense of foreboding and the stress of waiting. This march may be no bad thing: a little exercise for the heart! The word was passed down: sing! Private First Class Solti—a stocky, fresh-faced Magyar—began singing in a splendid, clear voice. I murmured the words along with him:

A mulberry tree stands in my yard
And a brown maid gathers its leaves
Gather them, maid, to rest my head
For I know that I die for my home.[1]

Not exactly an optimistic song. Many put on a brave face and sang along with Solti, but most of the men were sunk in thought.

Silence once more. Only the rhythmical clump of two thousand heavy hobnailed boots caused the air, bathed in sparkling sunlight, to quiver.

Kovács, the company commander, rode up alongside. "We're passing through Hungary's loveliest landscape," he called down to me.

"I've brought along a map, Captain. I find travel all the more enjoyable with a map."

"Very good. I'll borrow it from you."

I took it at once from my bread bag. "Here you are, sir."

He accepted it with thanks and rode on to the front of the company. From there I heard the command as it rippled back from the head of the regiment: "Halt! Ten minutes' rest! Fall out to the right!"

Ten minutes. If only someone would order right-about-turn. I undid the straps of my knapsack. Under it, I was already sweating. I lay back on the bank of the roadside ditch. The others gathered round and lay down. Sérsits conferred with the battalion and company commanders. I stripped grass stalks and nibbled the tender ends, just as I used to do in peacetime.

Osztermann sat silently, his legs crossed. Földes sat down. "It's all right so far. If it goes on like this, it won't be too bad."

"You can get used to any shit," growled Kovács. "And we may have to."

"My old life seems so far away now, it could as well have been in another world."

"Anyone know a good joke?"

"Come on, Földes!"

"Cohen lives opposites the Weisses. One day he looks out of the window with his opera glasses and sees Mrs. Weiss in a state of intimate undress cavorting with a man. Next day, he bumps into Weiss. 'Look here, Weiss. If the two of you want to fool around, at least pull the blind down! I could see everything again yesterday.' Weiss replies. 'Haha! Do you know what? I wasn't even at home yesterday.'"

Osztermann didn't laugh, but stared off into the distance.

"Kit on! Fall in!" The order rang out. We assembled into units and the column set off towards Nagyvászony. We were passing through a wood. The beauty of nature in August reigned everywhere. The boughs were a deep green, but the sprigs of barberry, the wild rose hips and the leaves of the sumac were already glowing in flaming colors of carmine, cinnabar, minium, and orange. Beauty before death, for autumn and decay were coming. In the meadows and fields, nothing but stubble and fine ploughed soil, the stalks of maize left tied into bundles. Subjects for landscapes: the colors from burnt sienna and ochre to gray umber. Marvelous colors in the shadows.

We had been marching for three hours. Monotony was setting in. Gradually, one was starting to put one leg in front of the other without thinking, without the exercise of will. The brain rested, as if some foreign body had been inserted into the cavity of the skull. External stimuli find their way infrequently to momentary snatches of awareness. An old peasant by the roadside, leaning against a tree at the edge of his field, watches us pass. Now there was something I hadn't seen before. Peasants don't usually cry.

Shouting and swearing from up ahead. A cow was determined to push its way through the column. A terrified boy, the cowherd, was whacking it. Its bones resounded under the blows.

Then on again. Nothing. No one was singing now.

"Rest break! Lunch! Boots off! Straighten out your foot bindings and socks!"

All those dusty, sweaty feet: a pretty sight, and a treat for the nose. A peasant spends all day on his feet; he stuffs his boots well with straw and rags, and he's fine. Military boots and creased foot bindings chafe feet raw. Already, many feet were blistered.

By my calculation, we had covered about twelve kilometers: half the allotted distance for the day. I too removed my boots—the waterproof pair I had bought in Pest—and located, then shook out, a tiny piece of grit. How had the wretched thing managed to get in? It was the merest crumb, yet already it had raised a blister on my sole. I fished out the lard and rubbed it all over my feet. A definite improvement.

I appointed a good-looking Slovak lad called Jóska from my unit as my batman. He was glad to do it. Straight away, he went off to the field kitchen and fetched me a mess tin full of thick beef soup with marrowbone, and a piece of toast. I told Miklósik, the corporal, to find out from the team leaders if anyone was unwell. He reported back promptly: no one. Just in time, too, because Győri, the battalion's medical officer, appeared. In peacetime, he was a dentist on the Ring, and this was the first time I had seen him riding a horse. He sat on it like a well-risen ball of dough. His voice sounded different, too, from the way it did in the coffeehouse. He seemed bored by the news that all was in order.

"So I should jolly well think."

"Földes! Give us a joke." We lit up and stretched out.

"Cohen goes to see the rabbi. 'O wise rabbi, I need advice. Weiss is the same age as me, but he's always boasting about how youthful he still is, and what a great lover, and how, and how often . . .' The rabbi strokes his beard for a bit, and then he says: 'Well, Cohen, just say the same thing!'"

Raucous laughter. Kovács slapped Osztermann on the back. "What are you staring at? Laugh with us for once, damn you!"

The word came: Kit on! Fall in! The words of command snapped and rattled; then: "Heading Nagyvászony! By the left, quick march!"

The entire column set off. The bugler and the drummer took turns keeping time. There was a little more spring in our step, and one could even hear singing here and there. But the freshness soon wore off, and the regular, mechanical movement of legs took over. We checked the map: another twelve to fourteen kilometers to go. We could no longer keep up a four-kilometer-per-hour average. The

road was monotonous, with slight rises and dips, the fields to left
and right ploughed or bare, patches of woodland off in the distance,
here and there, a solitary tree; and one monotonous pace after the
other, maybe the twenty thousandth by now. The odd farmstead or
wayside inn; the occasional peasant cursing by the roadside, or children following us for a stretch. So far, we had not passed a single
settlement, but we must be approaching Tótvászony. We were, in
fact, on a plateau; fortunately, there were few inclines to struggle our
way up, but there was not much else to be said for it. The men's heads
strained forward now, and I gave them permission to undo their collars and hang their caps on the ends of their rifles. They were loaded
down, all right: a rifle weighing six and a half kilos, a hundred and
twenty rounds of ammunition, their bits and pieces in their knap-
sacks, bread bag, spade, hatchet, mess tin, rolled-up cape, and so on.
Twenty to twenty-five kilos.

Corporal Miklósik reported that Privates Grossmann and Szabó
were unwell.

"What's the matter with them?"

"They don't know. They just don't feel well."

"Tell them to go back to the sick wagons and report to the medical officer." I told him to warn the men that if their feet got dam-
aged, there would be would be an investigation to establish whether
it was due to their negligence; if so, it would be a disciplinary matter.

He saluted and turned on his heel. The march dragged on. The
clumping of boots was gradually turning into shuffling. Another
eight kilometers by the map.

Lieutenant Kovács came up alongside.

"If I wasn't ashamed to do it," I said, "I'd get rid of this damned
knapsack."

"Send it back to the baggage cart."

"Gyenes might give me hard time for it."

"Too bad. You're not practical enough."

I waved Jóska over. "Take this back to the baggage cart. Tell them
it's mine."

It was incredible how, having got rid of the thing, I felt as if I could fly. The poor squaddies didn't even dare to envy me: I was an officer, after all.

The rhythm of the steps was starting to break up. Never mind now. Another six kilometers. My legs were like pieces of wood, no longer attached to my body. Maybe they would just go on marching by themselves, even when it was time to stop. They'd have to shoot them off me. It was three o'clock and the sun was getting lower in the sky, but it still burned our faces. A village could be seen some two kilometers away to the left. Another four kilometers or so to go, then. The road unchanging. A line of low wooded hills off to the left, just high enough to block the view. Alsócsepely-puszta: three kilometers to go . . . two kilometers.

I could make out our goal now, a smudge among the fields. I passed word to the men. One or two of them smiled, the others trudged on somberly, their heads forward. Even the desire for a cigarette had gone.

The village started to take definite shape.

The bellowed command: "Short rest! Smarten yourselves!"

The men threw off their loads and sprawled by the roadside. Not a good idea, I thought, to stop so suddenly after so much strain: I had seen horses driven too hard collapse when they stopped abruptly.

Miklósik reported three more men unwell. I noted down their names and sent them to the rear. To hell with theory: I threw myself down on the ground as well. I was lying in grass tall enough to hide me. It caressed my burning face with velvety coolness. Ants ran frenetically up and down the stalks. They knew why, which was more than I could say. Even they didn't know, though, why men had lost their minds.

"Kit on! Fall in!"

I had Miklósik pass the word: tidy yourselves up, fasten collars, caps on straight. Let's not look like a defeated rabble! A little early for that.

Nagyvászony: a proper village, with people out in the street, staring children, and the ruins of a castle on the right. That is all I remember of it.

Couriers had marked out where we were billeted. Captain Kovács ordered reveille at six and onward march at seven. He had been in the saddle all day and now he stood with his legs so wide apart that you could have crawled between them. Jóska showed me to my allotted billet. A peasant family welcomed us in with wonder, kindness, and respect, and chatted away with each of us. Decent, fine-looking, well-to-do folk. They showed me to my room, with a four-poster piled high with pillows and an eiderdown.

"I'd like two things, dear lady: a tubful of cold water, and a big jug of milk curd."

Jóska made himself useful and generally conducted himself very well, bringing my knapsack and the rest of my stuff. Then they brought in the tub and a bucket of water. I chased everyone out, stood in the tub, and washed myself from head to foot.

I felt revived. Now for the jug of milk curd. I would have dived into it if I could. My parched throat and swollen tongue dissolved intoxicatingly with the pleasure of the cool nectar, so that I practically merged into it. I gobbled up the whole lot—more than a liter—in moments. Then into bed.

My hosts were also putting up my NCOs in the adjoining room, and I could hear a few muffled fragments of conversation through the wall.

"Do they mean us to go all the way to Galicia like this? What's the point?"

"God only knows."

"The condition we're in now, a pair of Russkies armed with slingshots would give us a thrashing."

I recognized Miklósik's voice, then Solti's, then Corporal Zsimonyer's; then a bedbug crawled across my stomach ... little bugger ... and then I fell asleep the way only the very young and the very old can do.

———

"Ensign, sir! Ensign, sir!"

Where was I? I tried to gather my senses.

"Sir, time to get up, sir! It's way past reveille."

Jóska's voice. I had to pull myself together. The damp eiderdown was well and truly twisted round me. I could hardly move. My clothes and bedding were soaked with sweat. I tried to clamber out of bed, but the bedsheet came with me. I could utter only an idiotic mumbling. Jóska held me up and led me out to the well, where I stuck my head into the tub and had him wash my back. All my limbs ached with muscle pains. Somehow, though, I was coming back to life.

"Lord! You're not going to wear those wet clothes all day, are you? Why don't you put some fresh clothes on, and I'll give these a quick wash."

"There's no time for that."

"It won't take a minute. I'll wring them out and they'll be dry by the end of the day."

I did as I was told. The dry clothes had the miraculous effect of making me feel human again, though I was embarrassed at the horrid mess I'd made.

"You're better off this way. Who knows what you could have come down with, if you hadn't sweated it out."

I rushed about frantically getting everything ready and gulped down half a liter of fresh milk. I exchanged a few words with my hosts and thanked them for everything. They wouldn't accept any payment for washing my underclothes or the milk; when I said goodbye to the children, I gave each of them five korona—the price of a pair of shoes. They accompanied me out to the gate, from where they kept waving to me as I headed off.

We resumed the march relatively smart and rested, resigning ourselves to a further stretch of some twenty kilometers. We were told to keep good order, as breaking step would tire us, and to maintain marching pace for as long as possible. This was all true; but once fatigue reaches the brain, no force on earth can compel men to stay in step.

Here and there, a song could be heard, and from time to time, as we passed through settlements, bugles and drums went into action; but the tunes were feeble, didn't carry far, and lacked conviction.

Then everything subsided and the march resumed its mechanical character.

"Short rest! Fall out to the right!" The men threw off their packs. I made them stack their rifles. They lay flat in the cool, restful grass. I drank half a mess-tinful of strong black coffee. We gestured at each other with our chins.

"Go on," I indicated to Földes.

"Right, pay attention! Old Cohen goes to see a doctor, because he thinks he may have diabetes. The doctor tells him to come back the next day with a urine sample. Cohen shows up with a huge jarful. The doctor looks a bit surprised, but examines the contents and says to Cohen: 'I can put your mind at rest. There's nothing the matter with you.' Cohen rushes off to a telephone. 'Good news! The entire family is healthy!'"

This was a big hit. Even Osztermann smiled.

"Kit on! Fall in!" The landscape was a little more varied, and provided some distraction. Miklósik reported three more men unfit. Back to the wagons. I sent my knapsack back too. I was a little bit anxious about this, because all my money was in it—about five hundred korona, though the closer we got to battle, the less it would be worth. If I copped it, it would be stolen anyway.

Let's see the map. Sixteen kilometers to go.

Captain Kovács rode up alongside us. "Report, please!"

The units reported one after another. He noted it down. Thirty-five men in the company not fit to march. He shook his head. Twelve percent. This wouldn't do.

He tried to cheer us up. "Look over to the left. That's Mount Szent-György. There's Szigliget below it, and Badacsony further off. On the other side of the Balaton, that's Fonyód." He reveled in the beauty of it. We enthused more out a sense of loyalty.

The kilometers passed slowly. The men dragged their heels. Flowers stuck into rifle barrels waggled crookedly, like green and colored rags. The men had drunk all the water they had brought with them, and looked out for wells and springs by the roadside as they sweltered. But there were none. Many of them limped, not daring to report broken feet for fear of punishment. There were burning patches on the soles of my feet, too. When we stopped for lunch, I put on a pair of thick woolen socks, which relieved, or reduced, the chafing. Just above the rim of my heel there was a fold which pressed horribly on my Achilles tendon. I tried to avoid flexing my foot as I stepped. Twelve kilometers to go. Halfway.

"Halt! Fall out! Rest! Rifles stacked, kit off!"

The men threw themselves down, feet burning and swollen. They removed their boots and fished out filthy, sweaty, decaying foot-cloths. Those who had spares wrapped their feet in them—their poor, blistered, raw feet. Now that we were lying down, we could feel how exhausted we were. We avoided even the tiniest movement, if we could. Some men fell asleep at once, arms and legs splayed out, while flies and insects, thirsty for their sweat, crawled about on them undisturbed.

The rest break was an hour and a half, half an hour of which was lunch. It was plentiful and good. The men ate half a kilo of bread on top, until they were stuffed full. We were down to a plod for the rest of the route. I took almost no interest in my surroundings. I did notice, though, that we were going over a level crossing. Tapolca!

My billet was in some clerk's or minor official's home. I was given a divan, whose wayward springs made twanging noises and prodded me all night. Nothing bothered me any more.

We were informed during the evening that we would not be marching from here. A train would take us to Keszthely. Hallelujah! One more stretch like this, and there would be no one to take to the battlefield.

5. DEPLOYMENT

KESZTHELY. Our reception here was less enthusiastic than the send-off from Veszprém had been. Excitement and interest had started to wane. I had rested and got some sleep on the journey from Tapolca, moving from the officers' carriage (an ancient side-door rattletrap) to travel with my platoon, forty-first in a carriage seating forty. I had a bundle of straw brought in and put into a corner, where I slept like a log. Szigliget, Badacsony, Lake Balaton, and the other beauties of the earth would have to excuse my discourtesy.

I was received with chilly formality at the house where I was billeted; secretly, my hosts may have wished me to hell. Fortunately, I felt myself under no particular obligation towards them either. I returned there only to sleep; the entire day was spent out in combat training, wading waist-deep in ditches, then slithering across fields in attack formation, and the rest of it—thanks to which the state of the company's uniforms and equipment made us look like defeated troops in full flight. My so-called waterproof boots had been deproofed by all the wading about, and now they slurped underfoot like tripe. What could I wear tomorrow? I'd have to see about some new boots and leave these with Jóska as spares.

Luckily, my little room had its own entrance, so I could slip in unnoticed and thus avoid all the obligatory polite chitchat with my hosts. I would tidy myself up and head out for a stroll under the avenue of trees along the Balaton lakeshore with two delightful girls from Budapest, one of whom had been a pupil of mine there. Sometimes their father turned up as well. He was a senior clerk at a well-regarded bank and was furnished daily with the latest information

from "reliable sources" which did not find its way into the newspapers. His face gleamed with shining optimism as he recounted our
glorious advances and victories, day by day. I've noticed that those
aged around fifty are always the most optimistic—fat ones especially. Older people are less credulous. By the time they're eighty,
they just wave it aside. "That's nothing!" they say. "Now, in forty-
eight..."[1] And they jut their chins out in pride.

This routine was, at any rate, more agreeable than the forced
march which had preceded it.

Our company commander, Kovács, took us, his subalterns, to a
photographer's studio to have a group picture taken. Him in the
middle, the commanding officer; his junior officers to left and right.
I sent a print to my parents. The memory of our farewell brushed
past me again.

Soon, news came that we'd be off to Galicia in a matter of days.[2]

The order came on the fourth of September: prepare at once, the
battalion leaves at noon. Entrain at twelve, departure for the front at
one. Feverish activity, frantically grabbing things one would need
and things one would not; goodbyes and farewells. The regular officers serious, some of them somber. The whisper went round: all was
not well on the battlefield.

The two sweet girls had come looking for me. We said our goodbyes. Their encouraging smiles veiled the concern mirrored in their
anxious eyes. Dutifully, I played my part and affected gallant non-
chalance. They gave me a handful of saints' pictures for good luck; I
was not to forget them, and I was to put my trust in the talismans.
One was a St. Joseph with the infant Jesus, the other a Madonna and
child, both of fairy-tale beauty and surrounded with lilies. One
might not have thought a poor carpenter could present such a well-
groomed ideal of masculine perfection; nor the poor virgin mother,
careworn from toil. I suppose faith can be forgiven for representing
the ideal as the height of human perfection; for seeking to depict in
terms of the most perfect earthly beauty those that it honors and

reveres for the greatest spiritual perfection. I put them away carefully.

One battalion to a train. A thousand men, with the necessary horses, field kitchens, and so on, in some thirty or forty wagons. A worn-out side-door carriage for the officers. Share it out between you! Our company got two compartments, one sleeping two, the other three. My bunk was on the floor between the seats, on straw over which I spread my cape.

The train gave a jerk, the carriages clanking into motion one by one. We were heading, over every sort of branch line, for Komárom. We clattered across points. At one of the curves in the line, out of irrepressible childish curiosity, I observed that two Class IIIe small engines, hissing and coughing, wrestled with the load that snaked out behind. Happy childhood, when I marveled at the IIIe as a miracle of technology! Elbows up on the window ledge, I followed the objects and the creatures we were leaving behind, as they receded from my life, and were swallowed by time.

Csambalik, the corporal, had been promoted to sergeant. His face, radiant with happiness, put the light of a rising sun to shame. Despite everything, joy and hope know no bounds.

6. INTO THE FIRE

RAVA RUSKA.[1] A burned-out station building, the sign hanging askew from the façade. Somber silence. The little town all shot up. My billet is in the abandoned living quarters of a Jewish shop, sharing a bare room with Földes. A scattered stamp collection on the floor. I was a collector too, once. I pick a few of them up. You can see they have been carefully handled. Someone looked after them fondly and took delight in looking through them: Where is that person now? Nothing special here. I toss them aside. I had these too. Memories of childhood.

"I've sent Jóska off to beg, borrow, or steal some straw."

We make scrapes, burrow our way into them fully dressed, and within moments plummet into oblivion.

Jóska rouses me. (He's better than Földes's orderly.) Fall in! The battalion on parade at the railway station, between the abandoned tracks. Gyenes, the battalion commander, surveys the ranks. I give my platoon report. He roars at me.

"Ensign! You will present your sword when you report! Perhaps you're not aware that you're in the field of battle?"

I yank my sword out, and endeavor to comply sufficiently with Regulations to stop us from losing the war.

Then we form up. First, Second, Third, Fourth Companies! In double files, towards Dabrovka![2] A deserted track along the edge of a forest. Sand, sand, feet, and forest. Turkey oak and pine, September mists, the dewy chill of daybreak. The area is devoid of life. Even the birds are in hiding.

"Battalion halt! Left turn! Advance!"

The entire line enters the forest. Make camp! The grass is covered in dew, which I don't want to sit in, so I pile some broken-off branches into a kind of stool and take off my kit. This is all that I have now, and I shall be throwing that damned sword away myself at the first opportunity, as it just gets in the way at every move. Everything else—my clothes, my paints, my easels, my favorite palette and brushes, my dreams, my plans, my loved ones—is behind me now.

The lookouts report approaching troops in close formation moving from Rava Ruska. A Royal Hungarian battalion files past in front of us. The Twentieths.

Suddenly someone shouts at me: "Kalifa!"

I turn and see that it's Lajos Markó, with whom I worked on *Jó Pajtás* magazine and who introduced me to Ödön Tull. A decent chap and a good friend.

"Piláf!" (How we came by these names is a mystery.)

We hug each other, and I walk a stretch beside him. The memories we share shine through the haze covering the past that has been torn from me. The Kairó coffeehouse, the Fészek coffeehouse, trips together, friends, adventures...

"You'll see. It means good luck, our meeting like this. We'll both make it back."

We go on waving to each other for a while. My head is down as I make my way back to the unit. Földes hands me a cigarette. This must be my twentieth today. Suddenly, we freeze, and stare at each other: "Did you hear that?"

"Yes. Artillery! Sounds like we're getting near the thick of it."

"Or it's getting near us."

We weren't the only ones to hear. A silent tremor of anxiety ripples through the crowd. That was how it still was, then. Later on, it would become an everyday thing, as much a part of life as a greeting; then, even more so. Eventually, the greetings were dropped: the guns took their place. This was how the burning of the world announced itself.

"It'll be the big push now!" Brave talk, but you can sense the suppressed panic in the voices.

"Did someone just slam the cellar door?" Laughter.

"But why was there that double sound?"

"The first was the shot, the second was the detonation. It was a high-explosive shell," the adjutant explains.

Gyenes has conferred with the company commanders. No fires to be lit. All kit to remain packed. We could be ordered to move on, or to deploy, at any moment. We're being held in reserve for the time being, but they might deploy us. Weapons to be kept ready for action and to hand at all times.

Kovács: "Form up! Check your kit again!"

We do this mechanically. We think of nothing: nothing of the future, nothing of the past. Only of what is, now. What's past is gone. The future could last five minutes. The only reality is the present.

Slowly, dusk begins to fall; it is September and, in any case, sunset comes earlier here than it does in Budapest, four hundred kilometers to the west. They light the field stove, as the descending evening mist will hide any telltale smoke. When we have eaten, we post lookouts, four hours each, and try to settle down for some sleep. We have only our capes for cover. We've come as if on summer maneuvers. We can't make fires because their light will give us away. We begin to shiver from the cold; the grass and sandy ground are damp with dew. I wonder whether to dig, or scrape, a hole big enough to lie in, and to cover myself with something. The sand may be drier further down. I make a start with Jóska, and several others take up the idea.

"What's this? Digging our own graves, are we?" It's Gyenes. "Let's have some soldierly fortitude from you!" He rumbles on a bit, then waves his hand dismissively and moves on.

I make a little pillow-shaped mound of the soft sand and spread oak leaves over it. It does quite nicely.

"Gather them, maid, to rest my head."

Night falls. Fog fills the deeper hollow ahead of us, lapping it like a quilt, and slowly swelling towards us. If it reaches us, everything we have will be soaking wet: these dewdrops can fall horizontally. I settle down into my hole, and after an initial shiver I fall asleep. In my sleep I can feel the shivers running along my back gradually strengthen into shuddering, and then into shaking. I wake up, shake Jóska awake, and get him to heap a load of pine branches on top of me, so that I can at least feel something weighing on me. All this achieves is that the pine needles falling from the branches drop down my neck and into my ears. I draw myself in as far as I can, but my shaking has grown into a palsy. I feel stabbing pains in my lungs. I get up and shake the pine needles off myself. I can feel stabs of pain in every alveolus of my lungs. I can make no sound. That's it: pneumonia. Just what I need now. Those who huddled together with their backs against each other, or who snuggled up together, as pigs do, and covered themselves with their capes, have done better. I lean against a tree trunk and brood on the unattainable joy of a fire for toasting bacon fat.

The firing has stopped during the night; only the sound of the occasional nuisance shot echoes through the hills and forests.

As dawn approaches, every depression in the ground is covered in dew. Boots are soaked through after a few steps. The eastern half of the sky turns pink, and the snare-drum rattle of gunfire greets the rising of the sun. Rifle fire can still only be distantly heard, but the artillery fire is closer now.

"Kit on! Assemble!" The hot black coffee feels like redemption. How glorious it would be just to plunge bodily into it!

In complete silence and with dragging feet, the battalion moves off again along the track at the edge of the forest. The path is delineated by no more than wheel ruts in the sand to indicate the way. Our feet sink into the sand, and we make slow progress. The horizontal rays of the rising, blessed sun coat everything in warm cadmium and lapis lazuli. Long shadows of deep lilac undulate over the hummocky ground. The heads of the marching soldiers, straining forward in mute resolution, are bathed in cadmium orange, the plasticity of their forms sharply etched by the purple shadows of their eye sockets. In their eyes, staring blankly ahead, is reflected the fire of the rising sun. They glare at life. Splendid subject for a painting. A guilty thought, and a useless one.

The sun's caress, the easing of the chill. Not a sign of the expected chest cold. It's a wonder, what the human body can withstand. In Budapest, I'd be sneezing as soon as someone opened a door and window at the same time.

The noise of gunfire is getting ever closer. Now there is no more forest to our left. The bare slope has a wavering line of figures across it. The line moves uphill, then breaks apart. Above them a few little puffs of cloud, like balls of cotton wool.

Suddenly a fountain of earth erupts; amid the flying fragments, three figures, limbs flailing. Then, further along, another cone-shaped fountain, men tumbling from it. Shelling! Our troops are advancing against artillery!

"Into the woods, on the double, and take cover!"

Sweat is pouring from us by the time we reach the trees, but nobody needs any urging. Who knows, I may even have sweated out that bout of pneumonia I was expecting.

The trees in the forest have been smashed to pieces. A rain of steel and lead has shattered their branches and splintered their trunks. A scene of desolation. Indifferently, the sun casts its life-giving rays, even as man destroys.

Report from the field kitchen: one of the horses has been hit. This despite the fact that, as reserves, we are outside the shell-swept area, which extends to three hundred paces on either side of the firing line.[3] However, this width is determined on the basis of targeted gunfire; whereas the Russians, it seems, are firing at random. The result is that the danger area is increased by a factor of three or four, or even more, which makes any free movement impossible.

Suddenly, there's a cracking noise from one of the treetops, and a limb as thick as an arm comes crashing down.

Then a storm of bullets. "*Fffew . . .*" they say. "*Fffew . . .*"

Then a knock, like the sound of a watermelon being struck with a stick.

"Get down! Take cover!"

The fire is coming from the northeastern side of the wood. The exhausted men scramble for shelter at the bases of tree trunks with astonishing agility, trying to shrink themselves down to almost absurd compactness. One thick oak has three men flattened against it, each trying to shelter behind the other two. Mortal fear expressed by every atom of their bodies. Fantastic, what fear can drive us to. How would one record this, how preserve the expression of these movements? I too huddle under a fallen tree trunk, making myself as tiny as I can.

Gradually the noise dies down, the firing ceases, and the men dare to move. As evening falls, only the occasional nuisance round breaks the stillness. We can light cigarettes only under the cover of our capes. I'm not sure, but I suspect that this is all that's keeping me going now. It doesn't seem to be quite so desperately cold here in the woods. Anyway, it looks as if it's trying to cloud over. The full moon shines white as paper, its edge without definition.

Tension stops us from feeling our exhaustion; and anyway, word goes round: we're going into the line. Sure enough, the order comes. Form up into firing lines, weapons at the ready. We move off through the wood.

My wretched sword keeps snagging in the undergrowth, and I trip over it. Damn this thing! I wrench it off and hang it around my neck.

The wreckage of the forest gets worse and worse. We move forward, over hedge and ditch, across a width of about a thousand paces. Sometimes the lines clump together, sometimes they get spaced wider apart, but however careful we are, the snapping of twigs and the shuffling sounds of movement through the undergrowth generate a particular kind of muffled noise. I'm leading my platoon, with Földes to my right. The sergeant follows behind the firing lines.[4] The trees ever more shattered; here and there, piles of rags, the dead, weapons by the hundred strewn about. I pick one up in the moonlight and sling it over my shoulder. In my nervous excitement, I don't feel its weight.

I pass a dead man lying on his back. A Royal Hungarian. After a moment's hesitation I bend down quickly, unclasp his ammunition pouches, and buckle them round my waist. One of them is empty. I'll get some cartridges for it.

Piles of discarded rifles lie all around. Földes follows my example.

All Mannlichers.[5] Our weapons. Ghastly! What has happened here? It looks as if we've been sent to plug the gap left by some enormous rout.

How can all these rifles have been thrown away? I pick one up. The bolt is jammed solid. I take care in case it goes off in my hands. I pick up another. I can just about move the bolt. So that's it. The Galician sand has got into them. Luckily, mine is still all right.

I pass the word: keep the sand out of your weapons, or you'll have nothing to defend yourselves with! Never lay them down, keep them upright! Földes passes it on to the men.

Apart from the sound of our advance, there is silence now. Far off, to the right, the rumble of thunder.

————

The sun is low in the sky. Ahead of us, light is thickening at the edge of the forest, turning gray.

The order comes: "Halt! Sit, weapons at the ready!"

I throw my back against a tree trunk. I'm in luck: this side even has moss on it. The gentle prodding against my knotted back feels good even through my knapsack. I slide down and rest the back of my head on the fur of the knapsack.[6] How I could sleep, like this, here in the woods, if it wasn't for the little matter of a war! And it's true, every living creature apart from us has deserted the forest. Maybe even the carrion flies. Lead weights are pulling my eyelids shut. I can hear everything, but I'm asleep.

"Well, Rotter's finally gone mad!" I hear Földes say. I want to ask why, but no sound comes from my lips as they move.

Rotter is a reserve lieutenant in Fejtősy's company. He works for a bank. He's an uncommunicative young man: at times he won't laugh, at other times he won't speak, or even answer. He is kitted out with every imaginable article of warm clothing, a little "field table" that he can hang from his neck, a folding tripod seat, and goodness knows what else. A schoolboy's idea of war. The squaddies laugh at him behind his back, the officers tease him. He associates with no one; he is in a constant state of fear, all day and all night.

"The lieutenant reckons his time's up!" says Private First Class Solti.

"What's up with Rotter?" I ask.

"It's like talking to a brick wall. It's no use. He doesn't answer."

I remember how my old nanny always used to say that animals can tell when their time is up, just as they know there's going to be an earthquake.

I stagger to my feet. Kovács tells us what he has heard about our situation. The Russians are up on the line of little rounded hills visible beyond the edge of the forest. Their guns have acquired range for the area we're in. Yesterday they drove our troops out of here. The same forces, with artillery, are ranged against us. Our field regiment is to the right of us. A major engagement is expected tomorrow. We're waiting for the brigadier general. Nothing but good news!

The platoon leaders get together.

"Well, we're in it now," says Kovács, snapping his mouth shut.

No one has anything to add. Osztermann studies his boots morosely.

Földes begins. "Cohen goes to see the rabbi. 'Rabbi,' he says. 'You are a wise man, I need your advice. We have so many children, and we keep getting more. What should I do?' 'Listen, Cohen,' says the rabbi. 'Do you and your wife sleep together?' 'Yes.' 'When you go to bed, eat an apple.' 'An apple?' 'Yes, an apple.' 'Do you mean before, or after?'"

The joke does not go down well. Kovács brushes it angrily aside. "Bugger Cohen!"

Twenty paces from us the battalion adjutant is conferring with Captain Kovács. We signal to each other to keep quiet, and manage to pick up fragments of their conversation. The lieutenant is shaking his fists at the sky.

"Damn them! They blocked legislation for the sake of these stupid national-language commands, and held up modernization of the army.[7] Now here we are, unprepared and outnumbered three to one. The whole brigade has a total of four 7.5-centimeter field guns. The Russians have twelve."

Then he drops his voice, presumably to say something confidential. Our company commander listens, his head lowered, saying nothing.

We look at each other uneasily. This does not bode well.

The captain waves us over. "Once it gets dark, we'll get orders to take up positions. I will expect you, gentlemen"—no more informality now—"to do your duty in accordance with your oath."

Tight salutes.

I tell my NCOs to keep their teams together, as they are responsible for their men.

About two hours to go before dusk. What is one supposed to do now? Pray? Think of home? Try to clear one's head? Or escape into sleep?

The brigadier general is here. Where is all the pomp of peacetime now? The band striking up the march? I only notice him when I see two silhouettes sketched against the darkening sky at the edge of the forest. One tall and thin, the other shorter, medium build. That's the general. The tall one is the colonel. The general is saying something; the colonel is standing to attention, listening to him, just beyond the trees.

The general beckons to him. "Come back in here, won't you? You're presenting a target."

The colonel is a peacetime hero with a gray handlebar moustache. He smiles: "It's quite safe, General."

"That's an order. Get in!" snaps the general.

The colonel's face turns to stone, and he obliges, without haste. Then they go on conferring, but only the general speaks.

The news that's going around about the colonel, incidentally, is that he intends to forbid any digging of foxholes, as this "leads to cowardice and undermines discipline."

The following day, he would stand at the edge of the wood again, and receive a direct hit from a shell. There was not a shred of him left.

The same fate was to befall Lieutenant Rotter, although the poor man would happily have crawled down a mousehole to hide. He knew his time was up.

A reddish light glows above the eastern horizon, and then a full red moon slowly rises: not round, but shaped like an egg. Its enormous size and monstrous form stretch our already taut nerves to the breaking point. Silent panic grips every breast.

"They're signaling again!" shouts one of the men.

They've acquired range. Their observers are everywhere.

I explain—as most of them have realized—that it's just the moon. But I don't think we'll wait for it to start shining before taking up our positions.

Kovács, the company commander, summons the platoon leaders. We get our orders: take up positions along the crest of the row of hummocks up ahead. As the most junior in rank, I am on the left flank. Our mission: if the battalion has to retreat, provide cover, holding out to the last ditch.

"Carry on!"

We all salute smartly; the commander, too, holds the salute for the full "three bars of the march." The ceremony of the moment moves me. For the first time in my life, in its greatest moment, I salute from the heart, out of genuine respect for a courageous superior: József Kovács, my commanding officer, who is to share our fate in the coming drama. Budapest's cynical mockery is over; there is no place for banter. He shakes hands with each of us, then we turn on our heels and go to our platoons.

I issue commands to my platoon and try to prepare them: an attack is expected by morning, they should use the time till then making dugouts, present the smallest possible target, keep weapons protected from sand, open fire only when ordered, and so on. If they can, get some drinking water! I form up the firing line and set off, directing the men with both arms. They follow three or four paces behind. Even with the men spaced one pace apart, the line is some fifty meters wide.

As I step out from the cover of the wood, I instantly feel exposed and defenseless in the face of fate. But this feeling passes. All my attention is focused on getting into the right position. Slowly, I approach the mound's rim. I signal the men to halt, and I go forward slowly. There were positions here before us. Weapons all over the place, piles of clothing, corpses. There are signs of hurried attempts to dig in with entrenching tools (one to every two men), and with bare hands.

At my signal, the men come up. I indicate the line, left and right. I occupy a hole thirty or forty centimeters deep; beside me Miklósik, the corporal, who understands a few words of Slovak. I immediately start to dig; for the time being, using a tin lid that I've found, as I have no spade. The sandy soil is quite easy to dig, and gradually I enlarge the hole so that I can sit in it with my legs drawn up without my head showing. I carve out a little sill, onto which I place my "Eterna" luminous pocket watch. Miklósik has brought me a cape he has found, which I spread over myself. My watch shows nine o'clock. Nothing is going to start before four in the morning. I'll do a little more work on my dugout, then maybe I can even get a bit of sleep, so that I can get myself shot tomorrow in a more rested condition. Just don't think! Things are as they are, best to get used to it. The Russians are human beings too; they're scared as well. Forget Cavadarossi singing "never was life so dear to me!"[8] Oh! Szily Pongrácz wrote to me, and I left without saying goodbye to her.

"I can hear movement up ahead. Someone saying 'we'll go this way.'"

"Keep listening, Miklósik, but don't shoot!"

I hear nothing, but you can never compete with a peasant's eyesight and hearing. I hardly dare breathe.

"Listen, Miklósik, I'm going to try to get some sleep now. Wake me at one, then you can sleep. Nothing's going to happen before four."

The moon will have set by then, and the sun doesn't come up till six. The dial and hands of my watch glow. I huddle myself up until I'm the size of a large pork cheese. Silence. Just the crickets chirping. What a contrast! I smile at it, almost bitterly...

Someone is shaking me softly. I look at the watch. Two o'clock. Miklósik, stout fellow, has sacrificed an hour's sleep for me.

I can barely get my numbed limbs to move. There's a pain in my right shoulder that makes me groan. I shift position. The cape that Miklósik has found for me stinks to high heaven. But who cares here about trivialities?

Miklósik is snoring away. It's not as cold as last night, although the sky is clear. The moon is a little hazy, though. I look at my trusty watch. Every tick shortens the time I have left.

The sound of movement from the right; suddenly, a shot, and another; then hell breaks loose. I can't hear my own shouts.

"Cease fire! Cease fire!" roars the adjutant, in a frenzy. "Who gave the order to fire?"

Impossible to say. Perhaps a weapon went off in the hands of some soldier whose nerves were at breaking point, and that set off the entire the front line, like a landslide. Including me.

He holds his head in his hands. "We've shot our own men."

The Royal Hungarian Twentieths and the Thirty-Fourth Kassa Regiment were in front of us . . . Horror!

Miklósik's voice: "Maybe it was the Kassas I heard talking in Slovak."[9]

Lucky we didn't fire. Frozen silence. Even the crickets have gone quiet.

"I can hear something, like a sawing noise," says Miklósik. He crawls forward cautiously. After a short while he returns. "There's another foxhole about fifteen or twenty paces ahead of us. There's a man lying on the edge. It's his throat rattling."

"A soldier?"

"A soldier."

"We ought to bring him back here, but then what are we going to do with him? Or we should call for a stretcher bearer."

"Who's going to find a stretcher bearer now? He'll be dead anyway by the time they find him. His throat's shot through. He can't speak."

"A Hungarian soldier?"

"Yes."

"Royal Hungarian Army?"

"I think so."

"Take two of the men with you and bring him back here. Maybe the stretcher bearers can find their way here."

"Ensign, sir, if we start a lot of to-ing and fro-ing, we'll have the Russians firing at us."

"But we can't just leave him there!"

"He's there from yesterday's fighting. His own lot have left him there. He was there already when we got here. We just couldn't hear him, with all the crickets and the shuffling about."

Horrible! Listening helplessly to the gurgling of a dying man! I should speak to the adjutant. I can't leave the unit, and if I send a man off to report, I'm not likely to see him again.

"Take him some water!"

He stands, unnecessarily, and creeps forward in a low crouch. Soon he returns.

"He's not saying anything now. I'm not sure he's still alive."

He settles down into his hole and pulls his cape over himself. Five minutes later he's fast asleep. Happy man! I ought to learn from him.

The crickets have started up again. Everyone round me is asleep. I look at my watch as the minutes pass, one after the other. I'm still alive. I can still use my hands. I can still see. Just stop thinking! Three o'clock. Perhaps I could go back to sleep, not be conscious. It would be no hard thing to die like that. Unfortunately, I'm too wide awake for there to be any question of sleep. My city nerves. Good job I left my sword with Jóska; I couldn't even lie down if I had it with me in here. I widen my dugout a little, scratching away at it; at least it stops me from thinking. Half past three...The hands advance slowly...Four. It's still dark, no grayness yet. The moon has set. The sky is misty with dewfall. Four thirty. A faint grayness.

Down at the bottom of the slope, a man carrying a bundle leads a cow; a woman, bent double under her load, leads two children by the hand. They creep along like silent gray ghosts. Some distance behind them, another man with a bundle. Poor wretches, fleeing through no-man's land. Then the darkness swallows them up.

Five o'clock. The sky is definitely getting paler now. Gradually, the silhouettes of clumps of trees appear to the left and right, framing the view like pieces of stage scenery.

A flash of light straight ahead. A howling noise above our heads, then the curtain of heaven is rent apart. Shrapnel shells![10]

Now all hell is let loose. Artillery fire in salvos. All twelve guns firing at once. It starts behind us, at the edge of the woods, and works its way towards our positions. So that no one can escape to the rear. Now and then, some answering fire from our battery, but they're out-gunned. After two hours they fall silent. Now their infantry join in with rifle fire. Our troops return fire nervously. There is nothing to aim at. They're hitting nothing but thin air. I try to give the order to fire only when there's a target. What if we run out of ammunition? But my voice is lost in the hurricane. I can't even hear myself. After great effort, I seem to make out some movement at about a thousand, perhaps fifteen hundred meters. I, too, use my rifle. I can feel the heat of the barrel even through the wood of the stock. The bolt turns more and more stiffly, until I can barely yank it back. It won't go forward again. Sand has got into it. That's it! Our men are hardly firing at all now. It might even be wiser to stop firing altogether, since all we're doing is drawing the Russian artillery fire onto ourselves. I hear a shout from behind me. Solti raises his hand; he's had two fingers shot off. I signal him to go back, but he has other ideas. He'd rather live without two of his fingers than get himself shot to a sieve. Regulations have gone by the board. It's impossible to replenish ammunition: two men are supposed to run along the firing line, dropping fresh ammunition as they go. I have no way of communicating with my unit. The men are pinned down, level with the ground, awaiting their fate. The Russians are using high-explosive shells now.[11] Our guns are silent. Salvo after salvo. They start at the rear and within half an hour they will sweep our positions. One can count the salvos getting closer and closer. Now! Now! Here we go... My ears ring from blasts that pin me to the side of the dugout. Not a scratch on me yet. The barrage rolls forward. Ten minutes. Then they start again from the rear. The continuous deafening explosions, the howling of the flying shell fragments have practically stupefied me. Beside me, between salvos, Miklósik frantically digs himself deeper into his hole. I don't think he'd respond to any order now. Then a blast quite close to me: something has hit my knapsack and I'm almost suffocated under falling sand. My sole thought now, like an animal, is to save myself. Utterly helpless, I give myself up to my fate and, with no emotion, wait for the end to come. I am reduced to a reflex; I no longer care whether I'm hit or not. I am completely cut off from everything around me. I have no idea how many are still alive out of the multitude behind me, or how many have run for their lives. Since midday, the only firing is coming from ahead. Dusk is starting to set in now, and the firing is becoming intermittent. The Russians must be certain that they've finished us off. Miklósik is still growling alongside me. He crawls over, sees I'm still alive.

"Sir, I can see movement up ahead. Don't you think we should pull back? Those are Russians. If they find us here they'll beat us to death."

There is only sporadic firing now. Slowly, I drag my stiffened limbs out of the hole and throw myself onto my back, my arms and legs splayed out. My heart is somewhere in my throat, and for the time being I lack the strength to move. Miklósik crouches beside me; I feel the chill of a metal water bottle pressing against my chapped and swollen lips.

"Drink a little, sir."

I taste strong *pálinka*. The first thing to pass my lips all day. My throat shudders as if I were cold, but I'm not. I think my nerves are jangling from the alcohol, and numbness slowly spreads through me. I try to order my thoughts. My pride as a commander stirs a little shame in me: Miklósik has borne it better than I have. Ah well! His nerves draw their strength directly from mother earth. I try to kneel and look behind me. Silence. I put my weight on my hands, like a runner, and give the order: Pull back! My voice is cracked and carries no distance. I jump to my feet, and dimly see a few shadowy figures stand up and start to run. Summoning all my strength, I set off for the top of the slope in a crouching run: we'll be safe once we get to the other side. A few steps to go. Over cartridge cases, scattered kit, dead bodies. One more step. The Russians open fire. They've spotted us. I only notice the two bullet holes through the bottom of my cape the next day. It borders on the miraculous that I'm not hit. On the far side, I throw myself to the ground. My heart is in my throat, trying to jump out of my ears. Slowly, I set off under the cover of a little gully. Further on, the gully widens out. I find a group of men, a corporal trying to pull them together. One of them, his face yellow as wax, has both hands pressed to his belly and is crying out. The corporal orders them about sternly, with little effect. They go silent when they see me. Perhaps they expect me to take command. They're regulars from the Kassa Thirty-Fourths. These may be the very men we fired on yesterday. It dawns on me that I'm on my own. Not even Miklósik is with me. (I would never see him again.) I drag myself further on. I have to clamber up the slope of yet another hillock. Freshly ploughed earth. I slide in the furrows on my belly, struggling on, one step after another. The Russians are still firing, but blindly, into the gloom. It gets easier as I start to descend the other side. I get to some kind of path which leads towards the woods, whose margin is just a few hundred paces ahead. I drag myself on, more and more slowly, and I stumble twice. At last, the edge of the wood. I see people moving about.

A voice: "It's the ensign!"

"How did you make it out of that hell alive?"

Two of them take my arms and hold me up. A hefty young lieutenant hurries towards me. He grasps my shoulders and stares at me in disbelief.

"Incredible! Is it really you? Come, sit down. We've reported you lost. The battalion pulled back at midday. I can't believe you're here!"

He lays me down on a mossy bank beside the path.

"I'd like some water."

Several men reach their flasks out to me at once. I drink voraciously. As I come to my senses, I taste *pálinka*, but I keep swallowing automatically.

"You need to lie down. Rest, get your strength back. Come with me, I'll take you to a good, deep hole, where you'll be safe."

The beefy red-haired lieutenant is from one of our companies. I've had relatively little to do with him. He's from Debrecen and, with his purebred Magyar air of bravado, I had him down as a braggart. But now he takes me under his wing with genuine, warm-hearted comradeship. He leads me to a kind of broad pit, deep as a man is tall, beside a solitary little cottage. It even has a cover made from tree branches. We climb down a little ladder to get in. He puts some straw under me.

"Now then, lie yourself down here, put your knapsack under your head. Here's a bit of bread and sausage for you. You eat that, get your strength back a bit."

I fall asleep with the food still in my mouth, though it isn't proper sleep. I can hear everything, yet I'm helpless, and through it all I am shaking continuously. It starts in my back and spreads to my arms and legs. I speak only once, to say I am very cold. He doesn't answer: he's sleeping like a corpse. Then I sink into oblivion, although I can still feel the shaking, but as if it were racking someone else's body.

———

A hand is shaking my shoulder gently but persistently. I stagger to my feet, swaying as I put on my knapsack. We climb out of the pit and set off to find the others. The shelling has started up again, but not with the ferocity of the previous day. Whether because we have got used to it, or because we feel safe under the forest's cover, we ignore it.

"Yesterday was dreadful. Out of your company, Földes was killed, Osztermann is missing, Kovács was shot in the knee—if he lives, he'll be crippled for life. Kármán, in Third Company, had half his thigh shot away. Your company commander had a heart attack; they had to carry him off. Your lot were in the worst spot. The heaviest of the fighting between Lemberg and Rava Ruska was at Magierov-Dobrosin.[12] They've broken through the front. The whole Army is retreating towards the Carpathians."[13]

Our task is to cover the retreat of the Third Army. What an honor.

"Are you all right? You've gone a funny color. Like pickled cucumber."

"I don't know, but I feel so weak, I'll collapse any moment. I think it may be my heart."

He grabs my wrist.

"Stop, will you! I can't feel your pulse. You need to report sick as soon as we get back."

We find the rest of the unit soon after. I hear a voice behind me.

"Ensign, sir! I've got your sword."

It's Jóska, grinning broadly. I am glad to see his healthy young face, and I clap him happily on the shoulder. I strap the sword on: this should really scare the Russians.

We report to Gyenes, the battalion commander. He eyes me suspiciously. He and two others are all the regular officers left. He addresses us curtly.

"We've incurred losses.[14] New units need to be formed from the remaining men and NCOs. There's an officer shortage. Senior NCOs will take over command of some units."

Under the direction of the adjutant, the men form up in twos; facing them, the NCOs. A small group of the remaining officers stand to one side. I lie down. One of the reserve lieutenants comes over.

"What's the matter with you? You look dreadful. You're not doing anything: a sudden movement could finish you."

At that moment, six shrapnel shells howl overhead. The line of NCOs takes a direct hit. A row of three topple over lifelessly, like logs. A fourth has had his whole head torn off. He stays upright for a few moments, like an enormous jar of tomato paste, then keels over. I look around and see that I am practically alone; everyone has run into the thick of the forest.

The whole thing has happened in a small clearing in dense forest. How they can target us with such accuracy is a mystery. The only conceivable explanation would be some sort of signal—smoke, perhaps—from a forward observer.

The officers trickle back slowly, Gyenes first. The battalion's

medical officer, Győri, appears from behind a tree and takes a quick
look at the dead. One of them is lying with his head towards me. The
top of his skull is gone and the grayish-yellow brains are showing.
Győri draws down the corners of his mouth and spreads his hands:
nothing to be done.

I go over to Gyenes. I give a soldierly report: I feel very unwell, do
I have his permission to report to the aid post? He looks me up and
down.

"There's no need to be so afraid."

I draw myself up as best I can, but my voice is weak and queru-
lous. "I'm not afraid. I did not withdraw yesterday. I held on, without food or water."

"All right. That avenue of trees there leads to the castle. There's an
aid post there."

I trudge slowly off. I must have gone about three hundred paces
when I hear the howling of shrapnel directly above me. They're shelling individuals now. With the last of my strength, I flop down by the
thick trunk of a chestnut tree beside the drive.

The next instant it feels as though the earth has collided with
another planet, and I am caught between the two.

There is a silence so deep that I think I have gone deaf.

As I come to, there is blood running from around my eyes and
from my nose, into my lap.

After a few minutes, someone tries to lift me from the ground. It
is Csambalik. There is a look of horror on his face.

"Sir, we have to leave. They're shelling the drive."

He picks up my cap. It is shot through. I try to explain that I am
hurt, but only a meaningless stammering comes from my lips.

The strong, stalwart fellow half supports and half drags me away,
my legs collapsing under me.

The aid post resembles a butcher's shambles. Screaming wretches
are being operated on, out in the open, on tables. They sit me down,
and a doctor inspects my head wound.

"You're lucky. One centimeter closer to your ear, and that would
have been it."

Hastily, they bandage me up and wipe the blood from my face. Someone lifts me up, though I still weigh seventy kilos. It's Jóska. He carries me up the steps of a fabulously beautiful staircase and into a magnificent chamber, where he lays me down on the silk covers of a bed guarded by gilded griffins—muddy, filthy, and bloody as I am. A second later, I am unconscious, either having passed out, or simply fallen asleep.

How long I remain like this, I don't know; although, at some level below my suspended self-awareness, I can hear, over and over, a rushing sound. Eventually, I come to recognize the sound for what it is: shelling. It no longer troubles me. I go on lying there, sunk in utter lethargy, until Jóska appears and puts an end to my calm.

"Sir! Sir! I'll help you get up. We have to evacuate the castle.[15] The Russians are coming."

Complete indifference has overcome me, a wonderful feeling of equanimity. Apart from a dull ache in my head, I feel nothing. Even the unpleasant sensation I felt at my heart yesterday has gone. Why won't they just let me lie here?

Jóska stands beside me stiffly, but with visible impatience.

"I'll bring half a mess tin of coffee. They're handing it out at the moment, but they're in a hurry now, they're packing up. You're going to be put onto a cart, sir. They're putting the non-walking wounded onto peasant carts. Please get up quickly, sir!"

Quickly! My face twists into a smile. The patches of dried blood at the roots of my stubbly beard tug oddly at my face and neck. I try to raise myself up on my elbows and then to slide myself off the edge of the canopied bed. I get to my feet, but my right knee gives way under me in an odd way. I just manage to grab hold of one of the griffins to save myself from falling over. With difficulty, I stand up, but I keep getting this strange sensation that my right leg belongs to someone else.

Jóska comes back with black coffee. I sit on the edge of the bed and drink about a quarter of a liter of it. I tell Jóska that my leg doesn't feel right. He moves to my right side and holds me up.

"They're saying that sir needs to hurry up, because they won't wait. They can't send an orderly, as they're being used to load the wounded onto the cart."

I can't resist the temptation to gaze around the sumptuous two-story staircase, and the upper gallery with its ancestral portraits, spanning centuries, in baroque gilt frames. We finally shuffle our way down to the bottom of the semicircle of marble steps. Downstairs there is a wonderful marble fireplace, tapestries on the walls, and paintings: huge Dutch still lifes with hares and pheasants. I may be the last person to see all this, if war lays waste to it.

I am put up onto a long, narrow peasant cart. I sit down in the bed of the cart. Leaning my back against its side, I gaze in wonder at the castle's fine façade. They load up the wounded, groaning and crying out, one after the other, until the cart is full.

"Giddyup!" calls the orderly.

7. BACK TO LIFE

THE CART set off, creaking under its unaccustomed load. Two shaggy-haired ponies strained against harnesses of twine; the sorry pair looked like two large mice. How could they cope with this load in soft sand? It was painful just to look at them. The Ruthene pummeled them, but they seemed not to feel a thing. Perhaps their thick coats absorbed the blows.

We left behind the castle's outbuildings, the farmyard, the stables, the strawyard, until we were ambling along a track that ran among fields, some freshly ploughed, some planted with horse beans. At every lurch, a jolt of pain shot through my head, and the rest of the wounded groaned. One of them lay beside me, curled up into a ball. I could see no dressing on him. He had been shot in the stomach. Beside me sat a man supporting a broken arm with his other hand to lessen the jarring.

Jóska walked beside the cart with my sword slung from his shoulder. My knapsack was lost, with all my underwear, razor, and soap, among other things, as well as my money. Truly, no more worries or sorrows now, since I have nothing!

They would certainly be evacuating the field hospitals, and hopefully transferring us to regimental headquarters. Or—best of all—to a Budapest garrison hospital.

It dawned on me now that I was alive, and thinking about the future.

"Where are you taking us now?" I asked the orderly, who was ambling along beside me.

"We're taking the shortest route to Lubaczow.[1] With any luck, we'll catch the last train for the wounded, which leaves from there. It's another fifteen kilometers, at least; three or four hours, if all goes well. That's if these little nags"—he nodded towards the horses— "last out till then. Though they do say they're tough. We'll probably have to unload the walking wounded, or we'll get stuck in this."

I looked out over the deserted landscape, and a feeling of calm came over me. The rhythmical creaking of the wheel, as it wobbled from side to side, meant life. Step by step, it was rolling me towards life.

The cart's cargo had gone quiet. The soldier with the stomach wound lay completely silent. A fly walked across his face and rubbed its hind legs together. It flew off, then landed again. Crows picked over the ploughed fields, as they did at home. I felt my eyes closing.

———

I woke suddenly: we had stopped. The orderly was talking to a Ruthene.

"Does anyone here speak Slovak?"[2] I asked.

Jóska volunteered. "He says there are Cossacks moving in the woods over to the left there."

"That's all we need. What are we going to do now? We can't turn back."

"We'll have to take our chances. It might just be a false rumor."

"Let's keep going. Anyone who can walk should get off. They can hold on to side of the cart if they need to."

Four or five of us resigned ourselves and climbed down, including my neighbor with the broken arm.

The orderly peered intently at the face of the man with the stomach wound. He called Jóska over. "Come on, help me get him down!" They pulled the poor fellow off the cart somehow. His curled-up body had stiffened, and they tried to straighten it out, pressing down on his knees. Then they laid him down, face up, by the side of the track, and scattered a little earth over him. As an afterthought, the orderly removed his dog tags. All this was done hastily: we must hurry. We set off again.

I realized that I was running a temperature. My face was burning and my throat was parched.

We approached a wretched little village. The Ruthene had come with us and he was chattering away. No one understood what he said, but that didn't seem to bother him.

"What's he on about?" I asked Jóska.

"Ah! That soldiers have taken everything they had. He's asking for all sorts of things. Cigarettes. I've stopped paying any attention."

My entire wealth consisted of five cigarettes. I handed one to him. He showed his gratitude.

"*Vodu! Vodu!*" He resumed his chatter.

Jóska translated. "He says we shouldn't drink anything here. This is a Jewish village."[3] I'd never heard anything like this before. "They don't have anything. And anything they have, they've hidden."

We had entered a poverty-stricken village of a few mean little houses. The streets were deserted; the inhabitants had retreated indoors, out of sight, from where they stole the occasional curious glance in our direction. One solitary Jew, wearing a kaftan, had summoned up the courage to stand at the roadside, holding out a wine glass filled with a yellowish liquid. I took it to be lemonade. I beckoned to him. Eagerly, he ran up to the cart.

"*Limonade?*"

"*Ja, ja, sehr fein.*"

He reached it out to me with a skinny hand. I took it gratefully and, without much analysis of the fluid's composition, gulped it down in one go. It felt good. Whatever it was, it was liquid.

"*Ich danke,*" I said, handing back the glass. He stared at me with an expression of surprise and disappointment. Suddenly it dawned on me: his motivation wasn't compassion towards the wounded. He wanted paying.

Rage filled me. Damned bloodsucker! He has the gall to screw money out of a poor wounded soldier who has escaped death by a hair and lost everything he had. I shouted at him: "Off with you! I have nothing!"

He jumped back in mortal fear and ran off, side-locks flapping madly, to one of the little huts. I had to smile: here was someone I could scare even in my sorry state. I had no idea I could still have such an effect.

Leaving the little village in its hollow, we slowly climbed to the top of the rise. In the far distance, back in the direction from which we had come, smoke rose in tumbling, swelling clouds, spreading out in a layer that blanketed the forests and fields; occasional billows pushed further up before they, too, dissolved and dispersed.

"The castle's burning," said the orderly, who was pushing the cart beside me.

The end of the baronial castle of the princes of Horyniec, of the art treasures and vast wealth, of the gallery of ancestral portraits and of the canopied, silk-draped Empire bed. *Sic transit.*

We had to push the cart, as by now the two poor beasts could scarcely keep it moving. I took out a cigarette and hunted for matches. Reaching into my trouser pocket, I discovered my trusty companion, sharer of my fate, the comrade that connected me to my former life: my watch. I was so filled with joy that I could kiss it. I had something, after all. Not just an object, but a true and staunch friend. I held it in my left hand and marveled at it as it measured off the seconds. It was actually running. I had no idea when I had last wound it.

The orderly clicked his lighter, made from a Mannlicher cartridge case. "Sir!" I turned towards him and held out the cigarette with my right hand.

"That's quite a tremor, sir. It's the head wound that's causing that."

I'd noticed myself that, especially when I turned in a certain way, the trembling in my lower arm turned into a positive shaking. If that was the worst of it . . . It would go away eventually. All that mattered for now was that, with each step, I was getting further and further from mortal danger, and for a few weeks, at least, I would return to life. After that, what would be, would be.

We crossed a bridge over some little stream. A rickety structure: I was surprised that it took our weight. The sound of clean running water made me so thirsty that I yearned to lie down in it. I had no interest in eating, but oh, to drink, and drink, and keep drinking!

"We'll get to a larger settlement soon," said the orderly. "There are troops stationed there, and we can get something to eat and drink. There's a proper road from there that will take us to Lubaczow, if these nags can keep going. If not, we'll get other horses."

The Ruthene carter watered the little horses from a pail. Each of them drank almost a full pail. Where they put it all is a mystery.

With the cart stopped, my ears rang dully in the sudden silence, as if I were hearing everything from under water. My throat was so dry I could barely swallow.

"I think I have a bit of fever," I told the orderly.

"That's very likely, but please try to hold out until we get to Lubaczow. I have no drugs or dressings here. Try to sleep."

Sleep would be a fine thing, but I had to treat my head as if it were made of glass. Whatever I tried to rest my head on would shake about, and the pain made my eyes practically jump out my head. I tried resting my elbows on my knees and propping my chin on the palms of my hands, as we trundled down the hill. Ahead, and to our right, a larger settlement gradually came into view. The orderly said it was called Basznia.[4]

A little further on, we did indeed join a relatively good, metaled road, and the cart no longer pitched about so much. There were woods to one side of the road as we got nearer the settlement. At the edge of the woods stood a guard post—the first troops we had seen on our journey so far.

The commanding officer appeared, and there was some discussion. The cart waited. Those who had been on foot sat down; they were exhausted by now. We could take a rest. They brought us food and drink, and checked my bandages at the aid point. But we could not spend much time here: the front was heading this way, and the last train from Lubaczow would leave at sunset.

We were directed to the kitchen to wait. A cow was just being slaughtered, five or six paces away from me: a small, dun-colored, peasant's milch cow. It was the first time I had seen this done. One man twisted a rope around its horns, passed it through a pulley fixed to the ground, and hauled the animal's head right down to its fore-legs. Another man took an axe and, with all his strength, struck the cow's forehead. There was a crunching of bone, guttural grunting, the legs quivered, and the unfortunate creature slumped to the ground. It was all done with the indifference of someone swatting a fly. It was really just a matter of scale.

A medic examined us quickly; he tightened a bandage here and there and gave me three aspirins. He shook his head a little at the man shot in the lung.

After a short wait, Jóska brought a full mess tin of soup with some beef and marrowbone in it. Presented like this, these ingredients no longer seemed like the remains of a living creature, but merely sustenance. Jóska had shrewdly asked for this serving in my name, knowing that he would end up eating three-quarters of it himself, as indeed he did, in addition to his own ration. I told him to find a bottle and fill it with water.

A medical adjutant—from a battalion of the Twentieth Nagykanisza Regiment—came over.

"There are no more horses. For two days now, there's been a tor-rent of wounded, retreating troops, and Russian prisoners heading for Lubaczow. The horses are all being used to transport the wounded. Any other livestock is needed for provisioning."

We were the last, which was why we hadn't been picked up. Lu-baczow was the last stop now, but that was packed; people were being moved on from there by train. There was an abandoned station at Basznia; that was full too, of those who couldn't go any further. We should go there: they were expecting some old rolling stock to be shunted up from Lubaczow, and we might get to Lubaczow on that.

So we set off with the two exhausted jades. We just needed to make it as far as Basznia! The man who had been shot in the lung had been taken off the cart. He was dead. They draped his cape over him. They would bury him later.

The little horses were reluctant to get moving again. Their noses hung down almost to ground. Everyone felt a burning anxiety, because if we didn't make it to Lubaczow, our fates would be sealed: we would be taken prisoner, or worse.

We managed to struggle on as far as the station at Basznia. Wounded men lay crowded on the platform; plenty of malingerers, too. There were goods wagons of every description standing on the tracks—but no engine.

As we clambered down from the cart, my right knee buckled under me like a worn-out folding rule, and I would have collapsed like a sack if Jóska hadn't caught me. We shuffled our way onto the crowded platform where, in a corner, I slumped back against a wall. After a day of being shaken and jolted, it was a heavenly respite.

The awareness of my own helplessness bore down on me like a terrible weight, alongside my impatient longing to get away. For a moment, I was gripped by a subject: a writhing mass of wounded men, sustained by the hope of escape, awaiting their salvation. In this case, the savior would be some worn-out engine and a few shovelfuls of coal.[5]

Every minute, some new rumor or counter-rumor—many of them born of wishful thinking—went round.

A railwayman came running down the platform, shouting out: "Everyone into the wagons on track four, quick as you can! Let the seriously wounded on first!"

A terrible stampede began. Human wrecks, the bloodstained, the helpless, the broken pushing each other aside to save themselves. Jóska wrenched me to my feet and I threw my right arm around his neck. He dragged me off towards an empty wagon and practically threw me up onto it. I crawled on all fours into a corner. Out of breath, he grinned at me. We're all seriously wounded in here, aren't we? Of course we are! Just try leaving us off! Outside the wagon men were shouting, crying out, and cursing in a variety of languages.

A shout of joy went up: the engine's here! An ancient contraption, coughing and wheezing, rushed past us, great clouds of smoke pouring up from its tall chimney, on its way to the rear to be turned round. Its proportions were rather like those of the little horses that had drawn our cart. Never mind! It has wheels, and it moves!

At last, a jolt, and the whole sorry procession began slowly to move, clattering over the points and snaking out onto the line towards Lubaczow. No one knew whether we would have to change there, or whether this train would take us on towards Jaroslav; but we were filled with hope.

A bit of straw under me, and my joy would have been complete; but I did my best to stretch out my legs, lie back on my cape, and fold my arms to support my throbbing head. An immeasurable sense of calm came over me, undisturbed by the moaning, coughing, and talking of the others in the wagon.

I'm on my way home!

Jóska was shaking me. "We're in Lubaczow. We're being told to wait here until we can find out whether we're going on, or whether we have to get onto a different train. They say the local nurses are distributing charity for the wounded men. I'll get out and see what I can bring."

I had a sudden thought that he might want to run off; but that would make no sense, because he would be fine as long as he was with me, whereas if he were caught doing a bunk, he'd be in trouble. He was gone for quite a while, though, and I began to feel uneasy; but finally he reappeared with a smile on his face, pockets bulging and a bundle of straw under his arm. God bless him!

He stuffed the straw under me and laid out ham, sausage, fresh bread, a small bottle of *pálinka*, cigarettes, and goodness knows what else, upon which we positively threw ourselves. The greatest gift for me, though, was the straw. I stretched myself out and even pulled off my boots for the first time in three days. Then I fell head-long into the oblivion of sleep.

Now and again, I awoke, and at Jaroslav I even looked out of the open door of the wagon. There must have been an army provisioning base here. On the way to the front, I had seen sacks of flour in vast quantities piled up into stacks, like cordwood, on land next to the station. Now, a couple of skinny horses were chewing on sacking, their whole faces, up to the ears, white with flour.

Sleep.

Rzesow. A large station. Jóska shaking me back to life. "We have to change here." To make movement easier, we took with us only what we had on us. We left the food. We could get more.

I was somewhat unsteady getting off the train. Jóska propped me up from the right. A guard on the platform directed me to the station command post. I reported there and was examined by the doctor. He removed the dried-on dressing and said something about infection.

"If you get to Budapest, go to the garrison hospital. You need to be X-rayed to see if there's any damage to the motor centers."

"My right hand shakes when I move a certain way. My right leg buckles under me sometimes."

"Yes, that's related to the impact injury from the shot, but it's not serious. From what I can see, you should recover from that."

I was issued with a travel warrant to Budapest. Nothing wrong with Jóska: he was told to report to regimental headquarters in Veszprém. The warrant was for Neu-Sandez—Eperjes—Kassa—Miskolc—Budapest.

"I'll take the bandages off so that you have a bit of a wash."

"I have no towel, or soap, or toothbrush, or clean clothes."

The doctor spoke a few words to a nurse. "But don't get the wound wet."

I was shown to a bathroom and supplied with all that I needed. A wash! Could this be true? And clean clothing! I was given that too. The undershorts were too large and I had to hold them up. Never mind!

"Don't be fussy, Ensign. You're lucky to have these." I would get Jóska to re-sew the button once we were on the train.

"They'll give you something to eat at the field kitchens at the stations."

It had been two weeks since I had last looked in a mirror, and I was somewhat taken aback by what I saw, even though the mirror had lost most of its silvering. There was not much I could do about the blood-matted hair around the wound. The blood dried into my centimeter-long stubble was blackish-purple, a dark *caput mortuum*.[6]

There were also red patches the size of ten- and twenty-fillér coins at the roots of my beard. They itched abominably, and I had been scratching them absent-mindedly, but had not seen them until now. Two or three days, and I would be in Budapest. I wouldn't report to the hospital straight away. The family doctor could look after me.

Now to board a waiting passenger train, and sleep. I would be going home by the same route that I had come. How different things had been then! Neu-Sandez[7] decked out with flags and flowers, bands playing, crowds of the curious, well-wishers' gifts in heaps. *Ave, Caesar, morituri te salutant.*[8] The champagne had flowed. Now, with fresh bandages, I made no impression, even though my head was swathed in them. When I had gone, bloodily, to report, the crowd had parted ahead of me, and a young girl had stared at me aghast, her hand clapped over her mouth and her face frozen. The picture made such a vivid impression on me that I could still draw it. Now, with only my bloodstained coat to hint at what I had gone through, no one was in any hurry to let me through. I had lost my martial glamour.

A passenger train was waiting and we pushed our way onto an elderly, but decent, first-class carriage—a triple-axle side-door unit—reserved for officers, where we laid claim to half of a compartment. I stretched myself out and, minutes later, was asleep.

It was nighttime when I awoke with a start. The phosphorescent hands of my loyal friend showed one-thirty on the dial. The train was crawling along. With my forehead pressed against the window, I could just make out the hazy outlines of great mountains, amongst which our engine panted along endless curves. Dear Lord, we were already in the Tatra![9] We must be getting close to the Hungarian border; perhaps we had already crossed it.

Jóska was lying on his back on the floor and making snoring noises not unlike those that came from the engine.

I got up and stuffed my cape under his head as a pillow. He gave a slightly dim-witted smile and promptly went back to sleep.

I had started to find myself suddenly waking from sleep, gripped by the urge to escape from something or other and get somewhere or other, and it took a while for me to realize where I was. The slamming of a door would send a spasm through me, and I would jump to my feet, disorientated. A cigarette then calmed me down. Apart from that, I slept as if I had passed out.

I sat for hours with my face pressed against the window's glass, watching the passing scenery. A stream to the right and, to the left, the vague massing of huge mountains, like a stage set; all that was lacking was the Valkyries storming about the peaks. Above their summits, the sky was beginning to turn pale, defining the outlines of these colossal forms more distinctly against the background.

Nature slumbered, seemingly indifferent. Everything moved forward in accordance with unchanging laws; sleeping or waking, every struggle, in accordance with its slow, organic, gradual, hidden evolutionary laws. Nature flowed on its course, impervious to the absurd behavior of men, their mutual slaughter and assorted acts of wickedness. The whole world was manifestly indifferent in the face of the life-and-death struggles of men: it neither took their side nor opposed them, but simply paid no attention. Let them get on with it. Let them reap what they sow.

I awoke to find myself curled rigidly into a ball, my nose practically resting on my knees. I gathered up my cramped, numbed limbs and stretched myself out along the seat. Jóska snored on without interruption. Happy young lad, full of life. He'll live: his wily brain will protect him from every threat.

The train was racing downhill. It was getting light and the line was curving its way through beautiful countryside. We were in Hungary now. My home.

I was startled awake by noise, the shrieking of brakes and a familiar cry: "Eperjes!"[10]

Eperjes: the oft-repeated stories of my father's youthful days here...Tears came to my eyes. I'm tired out. My nerves aren't right. I lay still and pictured Budapest, my home. I had left another world behind there, a hundred years ago.

I knew the way from here. Kassa,[11] where we would have to change trains; Miskolc,[12] from where I could send a telegram home. I'd be home by tomorrow morning at the latest.

Jóska clambered to his feet, groaning noisily, clearing his throat, scratching himself, and the rest of it. *Naturalia non sunt turpia.*[13] Then he gathered himself together and jumped off the train in search of some breakfast and cigarettes. It was a large station with a military command post, and there would be charity volunteers. Minutes later, he was back, with a load of cold cuts and a fistful of cigarettes.

My wound had stopped hurting; only the dressing tugged at it. My right leg was still behaving oddly. I felt unsure of it and hardly dared to put my weight on it. It kept buckling under me. I had stopped paying it much attention. It was better than being dead. It wouldn't stop me from painting. If only! The future was still a big question mark. The war was still getting bigger.

An "unfit for service" came past; we exchanged greetings and he handed a newspaper in through the open window. Report from the battlefield! Glorious weather! Battle-readiness of our troops unbreakable! They await the Russian attack from new positions, etcetera. It had evidently been composed by the armchair generals[14] of the Pest coffeehouses. I leafed through the paper, looking mostly at the headlines. How alien it was! How far removed these people were from the agonies, the mortal fear as shells explode around you, the marches that exhaust to the limits of consciousness, the mangled dead, their open eyes staring into oblivion. Yes, far away, and with no conception of the reality of war. Of being unwashed, with clothes soaked for weeks in the tired body's every humid exhalation, and so filthy that they stick to the skin; of lice; or of when a man gets scabies and itches night and day, scratching his tormented body until it is bloody.

The editorial and literary tables of Pest's coffeehouses were surely, even now, untouchable; "essential occupations." Or, if the worst came to the worst, they would see about positions in the military press office.

The New York Café: the lair of the "Ady-ites," where all the prat-tlers gathered round to worship the master.[15] I had heard that Ady had done everything—apparently, he even went to see the prime minister—to avoid the overwhelming terror of battle. Festering in the coffeehouses all night is undoubtedly preferable to a nice little bullet through the gut: leave that to others. In his poems, he sings of death, whilst delegating its practical implementation. Such excep-tional people were entitled to stay at home instead, and rot morale.

The company at the Fészek coffeehouse must be there too. Tep-lánszky in full voice, Egry[16] playing chess or draughts, then at mid-night they would all file out to the amusement park to play at hoopla or some other foolery. A rum crew! I don't know where Teplánszky found them all. With most of them it's hard to tell who or what they are. The sculptors, at least—Károly Székely,[17] Péter Gindert[18]— come from the Epreskert artists' colony.[19] But those who are sup-posed to be painters? Even among these, there are some who are "of positive value," from Benczúr's[20] circle: Mányai,[21] Mozárt Rott-mann,[22] Emil Papp,[23] or one or two of Tépi's intelligent teacher friends: Heiman, Kornis, and Molnár. But these only come in the afternoons. Egry regards them as philistines and snipes at them fatu-ously. Heiman fires back: "Seems that you and teachers have never got on. You didn't get to school much."

I wouldn't be going to see them, I thought. Not for the time be-ing, anyway. They would receive me with cynicism, with something along the lines of "the enlightened anti-militarist always finds the hidden way, so that he can get out of this mess."

Kassa! We charge in, as befits a great station. The Kassa-Oderberg line terminates here, and we have to change onto the Hungarian National Railway.

Kassa: the largest and finest city I had ever seen at ten years of age. My admiring gaze paid homage to the beauties of its cathedral, and I wandered its big-city streets in a trance. My parents had taken me to visit some relatives, who welcomed us with shrieks of delight and half-Slovak exclamations, their short vowels unfamiliar to my Bereg county ears, and tugged me this way and that in affection.

"Lemme look atcher, lil fellah! *Jak se mas?*"[24]

They rather scared me. Then the good *borovicka*[25] would be brought out. Fond memories. My old nurse was from this district; she never learned Hungarian to her dying day. She spoke to my grandmother in Slovak: "*Panym rodrena.*"[26]

Memories that, until now, hadn't counted as memories. My head buzzed with them. Familiar landscapes stirred them up in me; familiar landscapes that were physically unchanged from when I had passed through them on my way to hell on earth, and yet were different now. Something had changed. They stirred up memories of my former life; I felt connected with them by bonds of emotion, yet they turned their backs on me. They had no interest in me. Everything went on living the life it had lived for centuries, indifferent to what men did. Nature simply has no interest in the works of men. Everything went on in its own way, and would have done so if I had bought it.

Nature has equipped man with every tool, every facility, with body and soul, brain and strength. If he puts these to bad use, he suffers the harm, but nature cares nothing of this. Until he turns against nature: then it gets its revenge.

Such thoughts occupied me, and the indifference of the external world oppressed me. I felt as if I had been abandoned.

In the wrecked forest at Magierov, I had seen only a single bird: an exhausted crow sitting on a broken branch. At the sound of gunfire it, too, had flown off somewhere. "There are humans here, I must escape and save my skin," he had thought to himself.

I believe that the world would look on unconcerned if the whole of mankind wiped itself out. It would create others. They might be cleverer.

The further away I got from the battlefield, the more indifferent people became. Here and there, I encountered a few enthusiastic and optimistic patriots who would sound off about Hungarian heroism; faced with them, I too felt indifferent. But what could they have done? It was not malice that had made them as they were; it seemed that this was natural. It's one thing to hear about something or observe it, and another to experience it. The crow had the right idea. Faced with danger, he fled; he did not fight, except perhaps for food.

Save your skin! Which would be fine, if the enemy did the same thing. But he'll wipe you out if you don't shoot back.

Save your skin, because if everyone sacrifices themselves, there will be no Hungary! Shoot back, and shoot straight! He who shoots first has the advantage.

Save your skin! You still have a lot of painting to do...

My gaze alighted on Jóska, who was sitting in the opposite corner. He was watching me with a smile on his face.

"Sir is always mulling over something. Sir is starting to go gray."

I looked at his young face, full of life. He took things as they came, following his healthy instinct, smiling slyly and saving his skin.

We sat silently facing each other, a man-child full of vitality, and a twenty-nine-year-old graybeard.

———

I sent a telegram from Miskolc: arriving home, injured, at such-and-such an hour. Sitting by the window, my forehead pressed against the cool glass, I gazed out, now and then dozing off for a minute. I only half-registered the familiar station names. Mezőkövesd, Szinhalom, glad days of my youth; I recognized the spot beside the embankment where we had picnicked, so much food and good cheer, where I had raced with Zoli; Zoli, who had thrown up afterwards, Uncle Béla staring in alarm; the prelude to a tragic early death, and a family's collapse.

Füzesabony: fun in the station tearoom; music at night, local lads, pretty girls. All distant memories, and remote, as if these things had not happened to me at all, but were stories told to me by someone I knew.

Budapest! The train glided slowly in under the glazed roof of the vast station hall. Jóska bustled about, trying to grab everything. I owed a debt of gratitude to this healthy, resourceful lad; though I knew that this personal service had been an opportunity for a bit of bunking-off on his part.

My father was standing on the platform. I could see him, but it took him a little while to spot me. He hurried towards me, his face pale. I must be strong now. Optimistic. Act like a soldier.

In his wordless embrace, I felt his arms tremble. I tried to smile.

With his left arm stretched out ahead of him, he opened a path through the waiting crowd, which parted in alarm. One or two people stared at me, with what seemed to me to be dread and horror. Indeed, I could not have been a reassuring sight in my cape blackened with dried blood, my blood-soaked bandages, and the dried blood and festering, itching patches alternating with dirt under my week-old stubble. I doubt if these all made a very favorable impression.

Never mind. I was dog tired and I didn't care about anything. We got into a cab for home. Rest! Rest!

8. HOME AGAIN

HOME. The familiar walls, the familiar furniture, my room, my bed; everything had waited for me, unchanged, in frozen silence. And they would have come to terms with having waited in vain. Only I had changed here. My store of experience had been enriched by innumerable new impressions which were woven into my entire consciousness and would affect me—even if worn by the passage of time—for the rest of my life. The patterns on the familiar chaise longue's plush upholstery were interwoven with the bare stumps of the trees in the Magierov forest, by glazed eyes staring into nothing.

Furtive eyes gazed out from behind curtains quietly pulled aside in the windows of the passageway flat in the courtyard. The Markbreiters. The hefty old cobbler with his green apron in the background, his hefty good-looking daughter in front and to one side, younger sister of the caricaturist Henrik Major[1] and future wife of the poet Zoltán Somlyó.[2] They stood motionless, giving no greeting.

My mother, too, received me in silence, only her lips trembling with emotion. It was only later that she could say something: "Thank God you're here." Her voice was hoarse and unfamiliar. I did my best to sound positive and convince them that I probably looked worse than I felt, and that I had got off relatively lightly, as things could have been more serious. Right now, all I wanted to do was to get myself clean, put on fresh clothes, get into bed, and sleep. And sleep.

"I've called Dr. Thomka," my father said. "He's on his way over now. He'd like to see you right away."

"Can he wait until I've got rid of several weeks' worth of Galician muck?"

"Never mind about that. It may be better if he sees you like this."

My mother received Jóska without much enthusiasm; she seemed anxious. "Where shall we put him?"

"All he needs is a straw mattress at night, which can be put away somewhere during the day. He's a good, decent lad, and I've got a lot to thank him for. Let him rest here for a week as well. Then he'll go back to the regiment."

The doctor arrived in a state of rapture. The wounded, in those days, still held some curiously fascinating glamour, although that would soon wither. At first, he didn't recognize me for the former man-about-town.

He examined me from top to toe. He left the dirty, bloodstained dressing in place and advised me to go the garrison hospital in Hungária Street as soon as possible, where they would remove the dressing. He didn't think the wound was dangerous and he could see no inflammation. The only thing was my nerves; I had probably suffered shock. I must be careful, when washing, not to get the dressing wet.

As long as he didn't ask me to talk about the battle . . .

But I was in luck: I was not to talk much, but go to bed and sleep. He gave me a sedative.

For the time being, I sat in the corner of the chaise longue and leaned my head back. The little ornaments in the niches above my head rattled. My eyes closed.

I was startled awake by unfamiliar sounds. I jumped up. My father was sitting, petrified, in front of me; beside him, two men in civilian clothes shrank back in fright, their eyes staring.

"What are you doing out here?" I shouted. "There's a battle going on! You'll get shot!"

"Calm yourself, son! You're at home. This gentleman is your friend Lajos Markó's brother. They're asking after you and their brother."

Gently, he sat me back down and stroked my head. Little by little, I came to my senses, and tried to smile in my embarrassment, but the visitors withdrew, apologizing and keen to get away. There was a brief quiet exchange in the hall, then I heard the door click shut.

Well done. Now they'll be telling tales of how crazy I am. Oh well.

They must let no one in!

My mother was standing in front of me. "Son … son …" she whispered. They were starting to behave as if I were an ill-tempered dog. "Your bath is ready."

"Mother dear, please send Jóska in to help me undress and scrub my back. Better keep the fire going, so that I have clean water for a rinse after the main bath."

Oh! A bath! A bath! My poor, filthy body; my gaping pores; the sand and dust of Galicia dissolved into the dried-on sweat. Floating weightlessly in the caress of warm water, wiggling my toes, turning slowly in the smooth-walled bathtub, being clean again. My poor, battered head, which, because of the dressing, I can't sink below the water to scrub off the layer of sand stuck in the roots of my hair.

The bathroom had wonderful acoustics. I slapped the water: the sound rang metallically. Then the march from *Judas Maccabeus* came into my head, and I began singing the bass line, as I had done in the Lichtenberg choir, and the whole bathroom rang with it:

See the conqu'ring
He-e-e-e-ro comes!
Sou-ou-ou-ou-ound the trumpets,
Bea-ea-eat the drums.

First, the choir of children; then the entire women's choir took over; finally the mighty male choir. I remembered how the sublime beauty of that storm of sound reaching up to the heavens had suddenly made my throat tighten, and I had had to stop singing.

As now. Hearing the chorus, I suddenly remembered my fallen state. See the conquering hero …

Back to the here and now! I called out in a voice worthy of the chorus: "Jóska! Come in here! Rub my back with the soapy brush until it's red, then ask for warm, dry towels."

I don't know how I got into bed. I only realized the next day that I had had no dinner.

———

My mother came into my room on tiptoe, smiling, holding out a bunch of red roses the size of a mill wheel.

"Thank God! It's as if you've been renewed! Your father and I were so happy to hear you singing in the bathroom. Look what that poor girl has sent you! Why don't you like her? She'd give her life for you."

"Mother dear, please stop, or I won't sing again."

"But she'd make you such a good wife! Beauty soon fades, but a good heart lasts a lifetime. Sebők has sent a message, he wants to visit you this afternoon. You stay in bed, I'll bring you your lunch. Sebők won't mind you being in bed when he calls."

Dear, soft-spoken Zsigmond Sebők. For the portrait I did of him, he had worn a sober morning coat which accentuated his slender elegance. He used to arrive for sittings punctual to the minute, and sought to serve the interests of art with his disciplined, almost frozen, poses.

Sure enough, he rang the doorbell at four in the afternoon. He approached the bed cautiously and his eyes searched my face. The touch of his warm, velvet-soft hand radiated friendship and love. He sat down beside me and we spoke for a long time about the events of the war, which then still had the thrill of novelty, the experience of battle, and the vicissitudes I had undergone. He made careful notes, then bade me a heartfelt goodbye. The next day a full-page article appeared in the *Budapesti Hírlap* about the heroic deeds of "a young friend and colleague"; and in that Sunday's edition of *Jó Pajtás* a friendly piece, for the benefit of junior readers, about "the heroic Mr. Moldován."

———

Dr. Thomka came again the next morning to examine me once more.

"You need to report to the garrison hospital tomorrow or, at the latest, the day after. I'm not going to touch the dressing. As far as I can tell, the wound's all right, but your nerves aren't what they should be. For now, take the tablets I'm going to prescribe."

I attempted a joke. "Doctor, don't make me too well, or they'll take me away again."

"Well, better to die healthy than live sick," was his riposte.

After he had gone, I decided to shave to the extent that the bandages would allow. The razor tugged damnably on my beard, which was stiff from the dried blood in it. But at last I was able to wash at least part of my face clean. I felt reborn. Looking in the mirror, I was astonished to see a scattering of gray hairs at my temples. My first step towards old age at the age of twenty-nine.

Zoli turned up in the afternoon. He had traveled all the way from Beregszász on my account. He burst in with his arms spread wide and anxiety in his eyes.

"Look at you! You can't trust a word they say. I came to see you on your deathbed, and instead I find a strapping figure of a man. I shall report back to Uncle Béla and family, who were just as worried as we were. We had an announcement about you printed in the *Beregi Hírlap*. I'm very concerned, though, to see you looking this well: they'll have you back at the front in no time. You'd better stop eating so much."

Then he told me that Vincze Vass was about to join the Bosnian regiment in Buda, and was dreadfully afraid. If he and his wife came to visit, I shouldn't scare them. The family was otherwise well. Jolika's husband hadn't been called up yet. He himself, as county prosecutor, was still exempt.

It did me good to hear his voice and his witty, clever conversation, and to be reminded of the happy childhood we had spent together.

Next day, I decided not to delay any longer in reporting to the hospital. I called Jóska in and told him he'd have to rejoin the regiment in Veszprém. He should report to the command post at the railway station and they would send him on. I gave him a twenty-korona note, which was proper money, and said goodbye to the fine lad. I would never see him again.

9. THE HOSPITAL

I REPORTED to the garrison hospital wearing the cape blackened with dried bloodstains. This was for the sake of my parents, who naively thought it would stir some impulse of pity towards me.

A stocky, elderly, benevolent staff doctor peeled away the dressing which had dried onto the wound and examined me.

"We need to be careful, there's some discharge..." He tested my reflexes and gave a little wiggle of his head.

"Surgery first of all, then to neurology," he told the orderly.

I got through surgery smoothly enough. The X-ray showed no serious deformation of the skull. They swabbed and dressed the wound, which felt good.

In the neurology department I was taken to a crowded ward, the beds crammed so close together that there was scarcely room to move between them. I was shown to a bed with a bulging straw mattress, a straw-filled bolster, and a blanket. I was to lie down and wait for the doctor's rounds.

The patients in there consisted mostly of nervous "crazies," made both apprehensive and good-natured by their illness. I soon made friends with an extremely timid young cadet suffering from shell-shock. As I was making up the bed, I managed straightaway to knock the board from the end of the bed to the floor—whereupon, in his fright, the poor fellow flailed his arms about wildly, crying out inarticulately. Compared with him, I must have had nerves of steel, as the incident left me unaffected. A good sign, I thought.

Afterwards, we chatted. He dreamed of a little house on Virányos

Street, a tender wife at his side, in quiet and in peace. To this day, I don't know whether things turned out that way.

There was a young trainee doctor, and an even younger Polish-Jewish pharmacist. The latter made the most noise. He went on and on about women and his various escapades with them. At other times, he would bellow out, at the top of his voice, a garbled scrap of song that he had picked up God knows where:

Ho vot lubbly pannomuse ist
Pale ink in dis knockin'-shop . . .

(Oh what lovely piano music
Playing in the new café!)[1]

The young trainee was earnest and officious, but he was a good lad and, when the need arose, he would hand out sedatives, bromide, phenobarbital, and the like.

The most serious case was the Polish legionary. A section of cranium the size of a five-korona coin was missing from the back of his head, and his brain was exposed. He lay there like a block of wood, helpless, and now and then he made a kind of wordless sobbing noise.

A young cadet had taken a bullet through the shoulder. It must have smashed some nerve, because he had no feeling on the left side of his body, which he sort of dragged around with him.

A shot had severed an artery in another man's leg; it seemed that he also had hemophilia, because it wouldn't stop bleeding. He was white as a sheet, but in good spirits.

A third man had been shot through the face. His jaw was wired up, and he could only open his mouth to a narrow slot, into which he shoved his food.

Doctors' rounds took place during the morning. The assistant to Frey, the consultant, turned out—to my surprise—to be Elek Falus.[2]

He had been called up as a private but seemed to have found a good billet. It was certainly a stroke of luck for me. I saw him discreetly drawing Frey's attention to me.

"Are you the chap who, according to the X-ray, has nothing in his head? There does seem to be something left in there, though, despite the X-ray."

I would have liked to reply, but in my humbled state, the most I could do was to acknowledge the joke with a modest, appreciative smile.

"Heightened reflex; traumatic neurosis,"[3] he said, adding a few Latin terms. Falus wrote it all down dutifully.

After that, the days passed slowly. A new patient came in, accompanied by his family: a well-built, good-looking young ensign, an engineer by profession. His very pretty younger sister had also come along, much to the delight of the "crazies." He and I later became good friends. We would go out at dusk to stroll around the building under the bare trees. Leaning on a stick, he shuffled along slowly and cautiously. At first I thought he had something wrong with his legs. But he held out his wrist and I could feel, to my amazement, that his pulse skipped every fifth or sixth beat. This was why he took such care over every movement.

Later, the trainee doctor waved it away. "That's nothing! He can live with it. His heart can still be all right."

One evening, during our walk, the bells in the city began to ring. You could even hear the old bell in the Basilica. A festive clamor spread out like a wave over Budapest. As we later learned, the Germans had won a great victory over the Russians at the Masurian (or, as the squaddies say, "Ramasurian") Lakes,[4] and Kaiser Wilhelm had, apparently, announced to his troops: "By the time the autumn leaves have fallen, you will all be home."

All very fine, and a faint ray of hope. But according to the British, "the war has only just started."

Amid the clanging of bells, I could clearly make out those of the Carmelite church in Huba Street. My first year at the Academy and the masses there. Angéla. From a distance of ten years, a memory from student days to raise a smile.

———

The trainee doctor said the Polish lad had had his skull patched up with a silver plate, and would recover. He had regained consciousness a couple of days before, and now, holding him up on either side, they put him on his feet. He was a head taller than either of the orderlies. We were all genuinely glad.

These two weeks passed slowly, with their continual examinations, amidst endless moaning and cursing. But the one constant subject among men in their twenties is women!

Unexpectedly, I had a visit from Ducika and Klára D——. Silence, as attention was focused on them; all of a sudden, the crew became well behaved. Even the cheeky pharmacist controlled himself.

After they had left, a voice broke the silence.

"Yer eyes are out on stalks, mate!"

It was sweet of them to visit. They even brought me flowers, and their kindness bolstered my vanity a little.

Over the next few days, the Pole started to babble. He was trying hard to communicate something and stared fixedly at me. Unfortunately, I couldn't understand even the Polish of the Academy, let alone someone babbling in the vernacular. However, it eventually turned out (as someone could follow Slovak) that he wanted to hear some classical Hungarian. I recited for him what they say is the finest line in Hungarian poetry:

> Field of mourning, reddened with heroic blood; with my sighs
> I greet thee . . .[5]

I emphasized the meter and the rich modulation of vowel sounds. He listened raptly and apparently declared: "Beautiful!"

———

I had little appetite and was smoking cigarettes one after the other. I had lost a lot of weight: down from sixty-eight kilos to fifty-six. One night, sleepless with anxiety, I suddenly felt so ill that I thought I was done for. It was the same thing that I had experienced after the battle at Magierov. My cries brought the trainee doctor, who stuffed tablets into me and made me drink a glass of water.

"Why won't they give us any medicine here?"

"You dunce! You're not here to be cured, you know. You're here so that they can keep an eye on you, and see if you're well enough to get yourself wounded again. Or killed."

"Give it a rest," several of the men growled. "Some of us wanna sleep." Not much show of sympathy.

———

A few days later Frey gave me another thorough examination, from head to foot. Diagnosis: traumatic neurosis. "Six months' leave," whispered Falus out of the corner of his mouth. No such luck. Based on the garrison hospital's investigation and "recommendation" (whatever that meant), I was to report to the notorious Szepesi, commanding officer of the hospital of the Hungarian National Army, as that was where I belonged.

A well-nourished and strapping figure of a man, he received me with a piercing look.

"Get rid of that stick, and stop playing it up!" he barked.

Obediently, I put down the walking stick. Summoning all my strength, I snapped to attention, and marched the length of the hall.

He promptly turned his back on me, and scrawled something at his desk.

"Dismissed!"

I withdrew, not exactly filled with benevolence towards him or his forebears.

To my surprise, I was nevertheless certified "unfit for service of any kind" for a period of three months.

A quick farewell to my fellow patients, none of whom I ever saw again—apart from the Pole, whom I saw sitting in a carriage, gazing with interest at the mansions along Andrássy Avenue. I was heartily glad at the brave lad's recovery.

10. LEAVE

WHEN I got home, I could barely climb the stairs, even with the assistance of the wings of joy at my release. How could I have got into such a poor state? My unexpected shouts brought the Wattai children, and then my mother, running down the stairs in surprise and delight.

"Three months!" The stairway rang with my shouts.

"Thank God you're home again. Your father will be so happy!"

I wanted to hug and kiss my familiar things, each one of them an old friend. My bed, with the tiny carved scrolls I knew so well. When I turned to face the wall, it made a little squeak. Even this was dear to me. I should have investigated what was causing it ages ago. But let it squeak: it would not be the same without it. The bedside cabinet, its drawer crammed full of useful and useless bits and pieces. The chaise longue, with its little ornaments that always rattled... and so on. This was my home. I loved it even more than when I had got back from the front.

"You can forget about the war now," my father said. "You've finished with it. You did your bit with honor. Three months! It's a long time. The killing will all be over soon. The Germans are giving the Russians a drubbing. Kaiser Wilhelm says everyone will be home for Christmas."

Such soaring optimism had an opposite effect on me, though. Did my father really see the cataclysm in such simple terms, or was this just for my sake? I didn't want to hear this kind of thing. It only got me brooding again over the hopelessness of the situation. The Entente were saying that the war had just begun. I didn't want to hear anything about victory or defeat. Let me live for three months. Let me paint.

The first thing I would do tomorrow would be to go and see my studio in Dohány Street. I would shut myself in, run my fingers over everything, and then pick up where I had left off, tying up as many of the torn threads as I could.

One by one, I would find the things that belonged to my former life: friends, the Fészek, the *Kunsthalle*, the school, the girls I knew...

And I would get my strength back. Maybe not too successfully: that might be dangerous, although the word going around was that the high command had come to their senses, and were no longer wasting personnel with quite the same conscienceless indifference.

I stretched out along my dear bed. True, I had not done my usual bedtime exercises—a dozen push-ups with my hands on the backs of two upright chairs—but I didn't dare to try. I doubt if I could have managed even one. I just gloried in the fact that I had the world's finest bed.

Next day, I set off for the studio. The usual route, along Dohány Street. I still had the walking stick that Szepesi had forbidden me to use. My sense of liberation practically gave me wings, and I had to hold myself back. Easy does it! What if I were to bump into Szepesi? I wouldn't put it past him to revoke my leave on the spot.

I was out of practice with stairs, and reached the third floor somewhat out of breath. It felt like only yesterday that I had last been here. My tools, unfinished pictures, the drawing table on which I done so many *Dörmögő* drawings, the armchair. It looked as if Teréz had tidied up a bit. I must let her know I'm back. I leaned back in the armchair and listened to the sounds of the big courtyard outside.

A little girl was practicing the piano on the first floor. She always used to stumble in the second movement and have to start the bar again. Just... there! I was relieved to hear that, out of consideration for my nerves, she went wrong precisely on cue. As if it were yesterday. Nothing had changed.

I had the same feeling about the people who came and went in the street. Life went on here. They were starting to find the wounded men about the place an annoyance; they just reminded them of the war.

The ruddy-cheeked exempted men especially.

"So, old chap, you still here?" you might ask one of them.

He pulls a face, his right hand patting the left side of his barrel chest.

"Easy for you, chum! It's my heart!" And lots of Latin terminology.

"Of course, of course." You look a little skeptical. The economy needs to be kept going, and that requires the exemption of men in essential occupations from service. But this many?

A new joke.

Cohen meets Weiss. "So how are you?" "Exemptionally well!"

Enough of politics. I set off to wander about the streets, with no particular goal. I just wanted, like a humble little brook, to join in the great swelling flow of life.

———

Next day: "Make sure you're home for lunch! We're having a lovely veal stew with soured cream and *nokkedli*. And pancakes stuffed with curd cheese."

Within a few days, though, the placid pleasures of leave began to pall. A sense of somehow being cut off; a feeling, to a certain extent, of alienation, began to grow within me. Things could not just go on from where they had left off. I had been an atom in the great throng of Budapest; now, that tie was starting to loosen.

Wounded men and amputees hung about everywhere in the streets; and those on leave, who also carried sticks. The wounded received the most attention, especially if they still had a little blood on them; showing some interest in what had happened to them could elicit much useful information. The amputees didn't count for much any more. Even speaking to them was risky: in their bitterness, they would blame and curse everyone and everything— Almighty God, Franz Joe, and Pista Tisza.[1] There was little to be gained from listening to all this; besides, there was always the danger that they might fix you with their glittering eyes and ask: "Fine young fellow like you, how come you're still skiving off, then? Instead of pretending to feel sorry for me, why don't you go and give your poor pals a hand?"

The men on leave limped like martyrs and told the worst horror-stories.

I went into the art school today.[2] My colleagues rushed up to me in the corridor in delight and sympathy; the last few days hadn't been enough to stop me being an object of pity. Ervin was the first to hug me; then Ventróczi and his wife Rózsi Kész,[3] an actress in the Comedy Theater. Ventróczi gripped me by the shoulders.

"It's all right! I can see in your eyes, it's the old you!"

"So, was it worth it? For who? The king?" asked his wife.

I smiled and shrugged my shoulders, as if to say: Well, even if it wasn't worth it, I can't exactly say that, dressed as I am.

Then a blizzard of the familiar questions. I really didn't want them to make too much of a fuss. A little way off, a growing group of the female students stared at me. I had been a hero to them only a little while ago.

The first body-blow hit me as I was going through the Oroszlán courtyard crossing. A pretty female model of mine stopped in front of me, her hand clapped to her mouth.

"Where did you go? What's become of you?"

I received the second body-blow from the school principal, Ágotai.[4]

I knew, as soon as I entered his office, that I had been too hasty. I should have waited another week or so, while I got myself together somehow.

He greeted me with cool courtesy and sat me down beside his desk. He examined me piercingly through hypnotic pale eyes while I spoke. I began to feel unwell. I could feel the blood draining from my face and I had to grip the arm of the chair.

"It's clear that you need to report to the chief medical officer. I can see for myself that you are not fit, at present, for work. The question is: Will you be fit to perform your duties at some point in the future?"

I had counted on everything but this.

I had expected, at least, some sort of encouragement and reassurance. I had not expected him to hit me right between the eyes with what a useless piece of junk I was.

I stood up and said nothing. I clicked my heels in military fashion, turned, and left, passing colleagues as they stared at me and attempting a smile for the students as they opened a way for me. I returned home with a bitter heart.

"My wages, the sun on my breast; my clothes, the ragged cloud."[5]

———

The chief medical officer walked nervously up and down his spacious receiving room, which was filled with hothouse plants.

"Look here, this isn't a matter that can be decided straight away. I've never come across this situation before, where someone found unfit for military service as a result of having been wounded in action has his pay stopped in consequence; then the individual concerned says to the civilian authority that, as he is unfit for military service, he should also be excused from service in his civilian employment, on full pay."

"I didn't say it was an everyday situation. Neither is war. This is extremely unfair. Having put my life on the line so others can go on living theirs in uninterrupted peace and quiet, I feel that I deserve better. They've stopped my army pay; and now, as I can't work, they want to stop my salary as well. Am I expected to go on the streets and beg?"

He stood rigidly before me. "If it wasn't out of consideration for your injury, and the fact that it was received in the service of your country, you'd get a reprimand for that."

"A reprimand? Well, that was worth fighting and suffering for!"

I saw that my boldness had taken him aback. He put a hand on my shoulder, and his voice became quiet and soothing.

"Please, calm yourself. You have to understand that yours is not the only case in which this question will arise. I'm going to have to discuss it with the senior legal officer, and instructions will need to be issued to the city council to regulate such cases. The department responsible for your school will shortly be notified of arrangements as far as you are concerned."

He gave a nod of the head to indicate that our interview was at an end.

Inwardly shaking, consumed by bitterness, I wandered aimlessly. It was a long time before I was able to consider the matter calmly. I realized that if he, an official, had no option but to speak as he did, then there must be, somewhere, a great injustice—at any rate, inhumanity. Sometimes, the letter of the law can kill.

Anyway, this was the third body-blow. Unfortunately, it was not to be my last.

A few days later, I received notification from the mayor's office that it had been noted that I had reported for work, but that—having regard to the fact that I had been wounded in action and, in particular, the severity of my injuries—I would be placed on unpaid leave.

One evening Géza Gl——'s wife, Inczi, turned up. She was a beautiful little thing with sparkling eyes and a perfectly formed row of teeth. I walked her home and she invited me to tea. I went the next day. Géza was at the front with the field postal service. She was charming, and cheered me up. I felt good.

Then she sat down at the piano and played several really lovely atmospheric recent songs of wartime.

Now the swallows all have flown
Over dales and hills
May the world, when they return,
Be freed from all these ills.

May men's blood and tears no more
Flow into the burn
When the springtime comes again
And swallows all return.

One of the loveliest was "The Map." Though a little sentimental, their melodies and words caught the romance of war. In another, a private finds himself among the beau monde in Váczi Street and propositions a beautiful "ladyship." "Let me be happy just this once, yerladyship; tomorrow morning, I'm marching off to war." Her ladyship is outraged and tells him to get lost. Social injustice!

I took a turn at the piano and sang one of the most beautiful of the soldiers' songs:

> A mulberry tree stands in my yard
> And a brown maid gathers its leaves
> Gather them, maid, to rest my head
> For I know that I die for my home.

Then another:

> I wander full of sadness
> Among these hills so dark
> Nothing, nothing can assuage
> This ache that fills my heart.

Then:

> To my dear old father,
> To my darling mother,
> To my pretty sweetheart,
> I write this letter
> I write this letter.

I was sitting next to her and suddenly I kissed her hand. Then her arm. Perhaps I should not have done that. She bent her head forward, and I could feel the glow of her face . . .

Géza was at the front, where everything is forgiven.

———

Over the next few days I decided to continue gallivanting about the city. I wanted to live with the possibility that I could free myself from all ties and lead a completely independent existence.

I went up to the studio less and less. I paid a visit to my neighbor there, Baroness Splényi. She received me warmly and kindly, and asked after everything. I told her the whole story, as I had done a hundred times by now. No one saw much of Adrienne; she was working as a volunteer nurse now. And a casual mention of someone new: Márton Lovászi. I was a little surprised; but there were other fish in the sea ...

Later on, Valér Ferenczy came in. Not having been a soldier, he observed me and listened to my remarks on the war with a certain detachment and a distinct lack of interest. It is, I suppose, under-standable that even someone who sees and hears a thing should place a different importance on it from someone who has actually experienced it as well. One has to take account of this; and also of the fact that suffering and the fear of death—indeed, death itself—look different from the perspective of the hinterland than they do to someone taking part. Gradually, I was beginning to see the un-adorned and harsh reality behind all the sympathy and the solemn extolling of heroism: "I'm glad you're back, but I'm even gladder that I didn't go, and I'll do whatever it takes not to go." Below the surface and despite all show to the contrary, the reality was that everyone had become engaged in a determined, sullen fight for life. It was a fight waged in complete silence and secrecy, but was none the less fierce for all that.

Those who had escaped death or physical ruin thought: I've done my bit, now it's the turn of those who, so far, have sat at home and enjoyed the benefits of being "essential"—respect, making decent money, and the favors of the swelling numbers of women hungry for love.

The others thought: I've never been a soldier, I'm not a soldier, and I'm not going to be a soldier. War is for soldiers. We have plenty to complain about too.

I felt that I was on the right lines in seeing this silent struggle as explaining the sense of alienation that grew within me day by day, dissolving the ties between me and the old Budapest.

I had another neighbor at the studio, Móricz Sándor. He had gone away; no one knew where. Inspired by the success I had had with some of my large compositions, he had had a go with one of his own, but with an Old Testament subject. It had turned out dreadfully—a crass, artless black mess. Whether he finished it or not, I don't know; I had gone by then.

I wasn't getting much done in the studio. I came up meaning to start work; but I hadn't counted on the fact that my entire emotional and mental world had taken a different path, down which, for the time being, I could make no progress.

Although my mind teemed with images of war, I didn't know where to begin. I had already made notes and compositional sketches for a dozen subjects, but they were confused and contradictory. I tried to distinguish them by leaving behind the bloody horrors, the limbless, headless corpses that are the real face of war. Not that: enough blood had been painted. However paradoxical it seemed, war created something. It brought about extraordinary qualities of spirit which could only be read about, in the cynical world of home, in the works of fervent popular writers. It is these higher feelings which make men human; they are what raises mankind, with all its wickedness, above the beasts.

I too had experienced examples of this: wounded men holding each other up, a soldier burying his fallen comrade, a Russian soldier giving water to the wounded, and countless others. I occupied myself with such subjects, but it was too soon for anything to come to fruition. At any rate, they were completely alien to the spirit I had found at home.

———

I transferred my perambulations to Buda. I found myself, at the age of thirty, revisiting my past.

I boarded the horse-drawn omnibus at Andrássy Avenue. I sat up in front, next to the driver. Fürdő Street, the Chain Bridge tunnel and Krisztina Square: four kreuzer. It was a journey I had taken many times when I started at the Academy of Fine Arts.

I always used to wonder how a pair of horses could cope with this monstrous contraption on wheels. But they plodded calmly on, even up the slow incline of the tunnel. In the evenings, the tunnel was quiet. The people of Buda retired to their beds, and only the occasional pedestrian's footsteps echoed as a single unbroken sound. Sometimes, if I found myself alone, I liked to call out the notes of a chord—C, E, G, C—to hear their individual sounds blending together and the ringing slowly, gradually dying away, like a distant chorus. I had got the idea from the interior of the Monument to the Battle of the Nations in Leipzig,[6] where a German singer was engaged to call forth amazing and varying chords, using the unique acoustics, from a series of individual notes. I felt like trying it again, but the clattering of the omnibus and the sound of the horses' hooves would have spoiled the effect. Besides, the driver would not have been impressed; at best, he would have thought "another nutcase from the battlefield."

The omnibus terminated by the Horváth gardens on Krisztina Square. Here stood the Summer Theater, an enormous wooden construction. I once came to see *Mignon*[7] here with Uncle Béla; he was so affected by it that his eyes filled with tears.

The parish church where István Széchényi[8] was married is here. Then the market, with the gypsy women's covered stalls. To the left, the Zöldfa tavern; to the right, another, the Vén Diófa; then the palace of the Karácsony counts with its vast park, a baroque stone figure of Hercules on its Krisztina Street façade.

Along Márvány Street. We used to live in the house on the corner, overlooking the enormous Jankovics park, the magnificent mansion in the style of the National Museum at its center. The third house on the left from us was the famous Márvány Menyaszony restaurant. Gypsy music could be heard playing there every night until dawn, to the chagrin of my poor father.

Beyond the Southern Railway Station overpass there were only a few scattered houses amid the fields.

During my second year at the Academy, I used to tutor Géza Prahács, who lived at the start of Németvölgy Street. I would go out to see him along lanes between fields full of maize. There was only one house on the hillside, the Szép Olaszn ő tavern. The constabulary lodgings were not far from here, the last house on Németvölgy Street. Poor Dr. Rehák used to complain about how often he had to go out there along this road, as he was the doctor to the lodgings.

I headed down the street, now less rustic in character. I stopped for a minute in front of the house at the end of its long garden, and smiled at the memory of how, at month's end, old Prahács—a chief inspector on the railway—used to hand me the fifteen korona, saying something (perhaps in Slovak) that sounded rather like "*netchy potchty.*"

I ought to go up to the Castle now and find the little Slovak restaurant for a pair of sausages with horseradish, washed down with a glass of good beer, for thirty-four kreuzer. Another time, though. I boarded the number fifteen tram—white stripe on a field of green— and headed home.

There I found Manczi and Vincze waiting for me. Vincze had been able once more to wriggle out of being called up.

Manczi took me to one side. "Have a word with Vincze, please. He's managed to get off again, but he can't hide how scared he is. It's getting almost embarrassing."

"Look, Manczi, dear. I'm superstitious. I don't want to stir up anything unpleasant with my pessimistic thoughts, but every time I've seen fear that goes beyond what's rational—when it becomes like a mania—the worst always happens. It might be some sort of instinctive awareness of the inevitable; or it might be that fear clouds the mind to the point where the judgment goes, you can no longer see what you need to do to save yourself, so that you behave irrationally, without realizing what you're doing—I don't think we'll ever know. I've wondered about this myself to the point where the thing I'm most afraid of is fear."

"He can't sleep any more. He's on sleeping pills."

"I think the only thing that works is to be tough with yourself and take things as they come. It's not all peaches and cream here at home either. I'll try telling him a few of my funnier anecdotes from the front."

I told him the one about the squaddies on the latrine. One says to the other: "My dear old Ma always used to say, 'Son, if you're going out for a shit, go as far from the house as you can.' Well, I've come a good long way now." The laughter sounded a bit strained. Vincze just smiled sourly.

On my return from Lovrana in March, there was a field postcard from him waiting for me.

"It's horrific. I can't bear any more. God be with you all."

I never saw him again.

———

I had decided against putting in an appearance at the Fészek coffeehouse. One evening, I peered through the window and saw the old crowd, diminished in number, sitting at the usual table. Egry was playing chess with Piazza; the others were reading or talking. Teplánszky appeared to be leading the discussion. I hesitated a minute or two over whether to go in. In the end, I did not.

Instead, I had the happy idea that I would pay Károly Székely a visit. Gyula Berán and Vilmos Szamosi-Sóos[9] also lived on the top floor of a fairly recent block of studios at the corner of Zárda and Zivatar Streets. Again, I crossed the Chain Bridge by omnibus, but I got off before the tunnel and walked along the high street. Above the church on Corvin Square, Szalag Street rose in an S. Baron Iplinyi and his family used to live just at the start of it, on the first floor of an old house with vaulted ceilings. I used to go there for parties. Adrienne always gave me a warm welcome. The parents honored me with their attentiveness. I spent happy hours in the spacious apartment full of antique furniture. Even with a slight squint in one eye, Adrienne was quite pretty; her kindness knew no bounds. With her short but exceptionally well-proportioned figure, she was lively in company, darting about hither and thither among the guests. The whole family was quite short, with black hair and eyes. It was said they were Armenian.

Walking up the curve of the street, I made a little detour, then emerged via Kacsa Street to the start of Zárda Street. I remembered this steeply sloping road from my student days, when it still had the stations of the cross all the way up to the Calvary in front of the charming little chapel at the summit of the hill. Here, at the chapel, was the top end of the ancient Gül-Baba Street that led up from the Danube side. Beyond that, there was only scrub, weeds, and bushes, with groves of acacia trees; however, there were footpaths that led to the Calvary at Óbuda, whose marvelously well-made stations stood on the way up to the Trinitarian monastery at Kiscell, then on up the hillside.

Once, when my cousin Zoli was staying in Pest, we had walked up to the end of Zárda Street; there, on the edge of an arbor of aca-cias, we lay in the grass, slightly drugged by the sweet scent of acacia flowers, marveling at the view of Pest. Looking up along the river, we saw spires and domes brushed by the rays of the afternoon sun, the rich contours of the Castle Hill sharply silhouetted in bluish gray against a yellow-green sky. The distant hills of Gödöllő were bathed in tones of orange, pink, and violet. It was a marvelous sight.

If I remember right, it was from about this spot that the Viennese artist Rudolf Alt[10] painted his view of Pest-Buda during the con-struction of the Chain Bridge.

Zoli had broken the silence. "This would be the place to buy a piece of land."

"Pricey. I hear they want twenty korona a fathom. I'm trying to persuade my father that we should jointly buy six hundred fathoms or so further up from us, where the Szép Olasznő is. Round there you can still get it at about two korona. But he's terribly cautious about that sort of thing."

We fell silent again, propped up on one elbow, the Gül Baba mansion with its four domed towers below us. Little did I know what a significant role it would later play in my life.[11]

Absorbed by these memories, I followed the stone wall of the Franciscan friary up to the corner of Zivatar Street.

I climbed the familiar steps and turned right towards Károly Székely's studio. (We called him "Carlo Siciliani.") They gave me a wonderful welcome. All three of them were there: Carlo, his marvelously refined and cultivated wife, and their angelically beautiful year-old little daughter.

"Well, I'm still in one piece. But don't ask me about battle. If I weren't already injured, I'd definitely make myself ill telling the same horror stories over and over again. Anyway, I'm starting to find that curiosity is becoming the new version of politeness here at home."

Noticing that this clumsy blunder on my part had struck a wrong note, I gave a mischievous wink.

"Real friends excepted, of course."

"You may certainly count us among those," Mrs. Székely interjected, a little evenly. But the mood quickly lightened.

I observed with genuine pleasure that they were all in good health and looking wonderful. We agreed that I wouldn't say a great deal, but was all the more interested to hear about how things were here at home.

"They've called Károly in to be conscripted. He'll have to join up soon."

This surprised me: he was thirty-four. Still, the army's enormous losses, particularly of officers, had to be made up.

"But as you haven't done any military service, they'll send you to the officers' academy for training. By the time you're ready to go to the front, the war will be long over." I was by no means convinced of this, but it had an air of logic, and its effect lightened the mood.

At my request, Carlo described how things were at home. The latest conscription lists had caused a great deal of alarm, and now everyone was trying to find a way to skive off. (I had read the mood right, then.) Had I heard what Béla Déry[12] had been up to? He had set up a so-called civil guard from the members—the younger members, that is—of the National Salon, for which he designed a uniform, with sword. Teplánszky had joined too, and showed up at the coffeehouse in full rig; Márton[13] had almost split his sides laughing. The idea was to replace the soldiers who were doing guard service here, so that they could be sent to the front. Lucky them. Déry appointed himself commanding officer. The military authorities immediately saw through the patriotic plan, put a stop to it, and called them all in for conscription. Half of them failed the medical, but the rest must be regular soldiers by now.

Most of the table at the coffeehouse was still there. The news getting back there had been very grim at first, though the "wartime sketches" that Falus wrote from hospital about his experiences more or less corresponded with reality.

Of the sculptors, Kornél Sámuel[14] had been killed, István Gács[15] had been taken prisoner, and Béla Karnya had been wounded, although—it was said unkindly—his injuries were chiefly to his nether regions.

The teachers that Teplánszky had brought in—Molnár, Heiman, and Kornis—had enlisted, but they didn't really belong to the core of the group anyway. There was more of everything for those who had stayed at home, and they were more interested in the opportunities which the situation presented than in events at the front. Egry just played billiards with Márton and chess with Mányai. The other day he had been playing with Rádna. Péter Gindert, sitting behind him, asked: "Playing chess? I thought you were learning to paint." Egry's piercing pale eyes flashed with anger. But Péter had stood up to him.

In any case, the chess was starting to degenerate. During the game, they would hoot or whistle loudly. Almási, who had tuberculosis, would come flying over in his coffeehouse frock coat: "Gentlemen, *please*!" Or else they would keep mumbling some piece of nonsense ad nauseam—"Liddle piggy's gonna dance"—which the kibitzers would repeat in chorus. Or: "Here I am with my drill—I'll stab you at the end of this poem!" Or: "Stabberola! What's he after?" Or simply: "Splat!" or "Splatterooni!"—endless drivel, spouted as if unconsciously, over and over.

Then out came memories of the trips we had done together—Brussels, Florence, Chemnitz (which we only passed through), and so on.

It was a lovely afternoon and evening. As we wished each other goodnight, we all had the feeling that saying goodbye was somehow different now: in the background, there always lurked the thought that this might be a last farewell.

As I was making my way home, it suddenly struck me: I would get away from Budapest. I would go and visit Uncle Béla in Sajóvárkony,[16] in the realm of quiet and peace.

11. SAJÓVÁRKONY

I WAS LATE getting to Bánréve, and there were no more trains down the branch line to Ózd. I would have to wait until six the next morning for my connection. Uncle Zoltán lived on the first floor of the station building, and I went to find him. He was overjoyed to see me. Since my aunt had died, he had lived here alone in the spacious service apartment. He had a reputation as a ladies' man, and his enthusiasm for the fair sex was undimmed. He looked a little worn, and his lanky frame was no longer as erect as it used to be.

"I've had the flu. I can hardly get out of the chair," he explained. I was fond of him, and impressed by the breadth of his horizons, his extensive reading, his fine library, and the fact that everyone on the station staff liked him. He would often treat them all, down to the last assistant, to a meal in the station restaurant, thanks to which they all thought him a great democrat.

Naturally enough, our conversation soon turned to the war. How and where had I been wounded? It hardly showed! What a dashing lieutenant I looked,[1] and fit as a fiddle! Our advance may have been halted, but we would win in the end; and how good everything would be when the war was over.

He still had something of the daredevil about him; his optimistic, life-affirming nature would allow no other conclusion. But, somehow, he seemed to have sensed all that I was thinking inwardly, but was keeping to myself—or else I may inadvertently have made some dry remark or other—because he turned serious. Perhaps he had expected greater patriotism from his favorite nephew.

"Well, let's go down and have some dinner, and we can save the rest for tomorrow."

The customary private table awaited us in the station restaurant. There was a general atmosphere of respect for the "guv'nor."

We ate a plentiful—perhaps too plentiful—dinner, and the wine flowed. Afterwards, as we were climbing the stairs, he stopped, gasping for breath and gripping the bannister. In the semi-darkness, the pallor of his face shone out horribly. Wide-eyed, he stared fixedly at me.

"We came up a bit fast," he mumbled. "I'll be all right in minute."

We started slowly up the stairs again. I reached out to take his arm.

"Leave it! I'm fine now."

During the night, half asleep, I heard him wheezing, short of breath, as he slowly crossed my room; slowly, so as not to awaken me.

I woke at daybreak. The deathly silence was broken only by the puffing of a shunting engine in the distance.

"How's the guv'nor? He thinks it's down to the flu; actually, he's got terminal heart disease. His doctor's wasting his breath. He still has a wild old time chasing women. He's incorrigible." The lady cashier circled a finger next to her ear as she counted out my change.

I didn't know then that I had seen him for the last time. The poor man would never know victory, or happy times after the war. His misbehaving heart just could not wait to carry him off.

—

My reception at Uncle Béla's was ecstatic, as if their much-loved nephew had returned from the dead. He was swift as ever to embrace me, and I felt the brush of his puffy, faintly sweaty face from right and left. I was pulled firmly in to his broad, full chest with such intense love that it felt as if I had fallen into a pile of cushions.

His housekeeper, Annuczi, hobbled towards me—she suffered terribly from sore feet—greeting me with her thin, rasping voice and kissing me.

I passed my viva voce on the war relatively easily, although, despite my best efforts, I caused some disappointment by not being a sufficiently enthusiastic advocate for the unshakeable certainty of ultimate victory. These people at home were amazing.

I was reminded of the great aquarium in Naples. For hours on end, through plate glass walls three meters high, I had watched a huge turtle, which must have weighed fifty kilos, frolicking with a ray. The ray measured about two meters across. With a grace that would have put the most sinuous dancer to shame, it hovered and fluttered. The turtle scooped at the water and, where it could, took palm-size bites out of the edge of the ray's wings, as one might break a morsel off the edge of a matzo. The ray presumably noticed this, since it dived swiftly down to the floor of the tank and, with wave-like movements of its wings, stirred up such a cloud of silt that nothing could be seen. When the silt had settled, covering the immobile ray, the turtle dawdled about aimlessly for a bit before sinking to the bottom to rest. As an observer, I looked on sardonically: Which of them would win?

Those who had stayed at home must have observed things the same way as I had at that aquarium. The possibility could not be ruled out that, had I remained at home, I would have observed the war in a similar way—through a glass wall.

I reflected on all this as I sank into a bed frothy with eiderdown. The room was large, with a vaulted ceiling and walls of stone half a meter thick. It exuded a sense of secure calm, and the silence worked on me like the deathly stillness of the crypt. I forgave them everything.

The only sound came from the door to Uncle Béla's bedroom, but that was no louder than a mosquito's hum.

I woke the next morning to the sound of clattering and rattling from the corridor outside. It was the stoker, laying a fire from outside in the big tiled stove in my room. I knew what would happen next: within half an hour the room would be so hot that I would have to escape. A peasant loves nothing more than an overheated room. The good stoker would make a special point of being friendly to me now. The hotter the room, the better the tip!

It wasn't quite so early in the morning, after all. Only the wooden shutters were keeping the room in darkness. Before long, we could start looking forward to spring.

The days passed. It felt good to rest. Every hour I would hear Annuczi's thin voice asking: "Aren't you hungry, Béla?" She really stuffed me like a goose.

"No, I'm fine, Annuczi. You'll fatten me up, then they'll send me to the front again."

"Oh, if only it would end!"

"It will, eventually. I'm just not sure it will do us much good when it does."

I applied myself to looking through the contents of the fine triple-bayed Baroque bookcase that stood in the vaulted hallway. One by one, I took out the perfectly proportioned folios in their banded leather and vellum bindings from the seventeenth and eighteenth centuries. They were mostly ecclesiastical texts, with engraved portraits of eminent churchmen. Superb, irreplaceable work. I doubt if anyone now could combine this degree of technical mastery, draftsmanship, mental discipline, and innate artistry. And these artists, for the most part, remained nameless throughout careers which were crammed with work of real worth.

A dying art. Only a handful of copper engravers survive, their skill displayed on the occasional banknote or postage stamp. They, too, will probably be swept away by the tidal wave of ever more rapidly developing mechanical processes. There ought to be a museum of graphic art to ensure that treasures like these are not lost.

One evening, Uncle Béla and I were invited by one of the local farmers to dinner to celebrate the slaughtering of a pig.

Uncle Béla—whose love of food was his undoing—was delighted. He listed all the dishes we could expect: fresh sausage, blood pudding, backbone soup, boiled ribs with horseradish, stuffed cabbage rolls with pork belly, loin of pork fried in breadcrumbs, noodles with curd cheese, etcetera.

Even without the etcetera, this would have been enough for me, and beyond my capabilities. How was I going to escape? Courtesy would require second helpings of each course. And then the insistent, deadly offers of more. And an endless succession of wines.

"Do I really have to go as well?"

Uncle Béla sprang to his feet. The settee creaked and groaned in protest.

"Please. You're asking the impossible. The man is one of the most upright and prosperous farmers in the village, and a faithful member of my congregation. He would be mortified if you didn't show up."

"God forbid! I wouldn't want that."

Forsake me not, O Lord.

We set off at seven down the muddy street, a good fifty meters wide, in pitch darkness. I thought with regret of my poor shoes— bought from Weisfeld—and slithered about stoically through the slippery mire. Every dog was quiet; Uncle Béla evidently commanded respect there as well.

Ahead of us, lit candles in the windows identified the home of our host and his fine family. He stood waiting for us, bareheaded, by the gate. The clatter of dishes could be heard from within.

As he led us in, three local gypsies struck up with a flourish, and the womenfolk of the house lined up in front of Uncle Béla to kiss his hand.

In its honest, artless way, the whole reception was rather touching.

The room was crowded with people. The aromas wafting from the corners and lively exclamations suggested that a good number of them had already sampled the delights to come, especially the liquid instruments of hospitality.

I took off my sword, thinking that the restriction of the strap might limit my capacity to cope with whatever portions might assail me. The host's brother-in-law promptly took possession of it. His face beamed and his eyes lit up as he held the thing between his knees and put his hand round the grip. The glittering gold tassel lay on his thigh, and now and then he reached down and stroked it rapturously. This was no small thing. He had done his military service years ago, and he was past his prime, but—especially in the old days—no officer's sword would ever have been entrusted to him. This was not just a steel weapon. It was a symbol. A gentleman was entitled to bear one and derived his authority from it. An officer in debt was "down to the tassels of his sword." An officer's oath sworn "by the tassels of his sword" was weightier than his mere word.

"His Majesty wears one just like this. It's what makes a man fit for court." And now he was free to fiddle with this sacred piece of regalia.

Uncle Béla sat at the head of the table, the center of much noisy attention. Animated, lively voices called out this way and that, one on top of the other. Prominent among them was the rasp of the host's stentorian oration in praise of the qualities of the defunct porker.

"She was a magnificent beast! Nine piglets she had in that litter. Slimmed down a bit after that, but she still made two hundred and fifty kilos. Her fatback's as wide as my hand"—he spread his fingers to demonstrate—"with twenty kilos of it each side."

Uncle Béla had numerous helpings of each dish. How could he manage it? A voice congested with cold began to drone from beside the bread oven. The womenfolk came round again, offering more. What should I do? I didn't even like the food much, especially their sausages, which tasted of lemons. Shrieking with laughter, they loaded up my plate with fresh heaps and gay abandon. The stale air swam thickly with the smell of freshly fried cubes of pork fat, a huge dishful of which was now brought in. Lord help me! The brother-in-law hovered at my elbow—the sword had created a certain bond between us—and kept refilling my glass.

Dear Lord. If only I could feel hunger once more in this life! Every eye was upon me. A hero had to be able to stand his ground here as well. What kind of hero lets himself be beaten by a boiled sausage? A soldier must eat to get himself good and strong, so that he can give those weedy troublemakers a good drubbing.

I felt myself turning pale. I was unpleasantly hot. My heart raced, and the sweat broke out on my brow. I asked the brother-in-law to open a window.

The fresh air reached my legs first, then my chest. I breathed it in thirstily and felt better.

"What are you letting all the warm out for?" shrieked the woman with the cold from beside the bread oven. She must have been expressing the majority view, since about five people sprang up to shut the window. That was that.

Uncle Béla now hauled his entire bulk to his feet. He was a quite an imposing presence, in his canonical sash and his cassock with its row of red buttons, like wild strawberries. An attentive hush fell, and then he spoke. There was a somewhat ecclesiastical flavor to his speech; he saluted the host and his family in terms that were larded with references to the Bible and its stupendous feasts, and the miracle of the loaves and the fishes, thanks to which all could eat their fill. There was something about the family being upright, God-fearing folk, and about the divine benevolence that made it possible for all these decent people present here today to share in the bounty of His blessings (courtesy of the pig), and so on, and so forth.

The polished tones of his mighty organ rang out. A couple of old women dressed in black sat, like crows, hunched on the bench beside the bread oven. One or other of them even gave a little sniff.

When the speech was over, the suppressed high spirits broke out again with elemental force. Everyone spoke to everyone else, and everyone spoke about something different. In all the hubbub, I seized my chance to lean across to Uncle Béla.

"I think I've eaten too much. I don't feel well. Can we go home now?"

He looked at me in surprise and wonderment.

"Let's at least wait for the host's reply. Why don't you go outside for a little fresh air?"

How to go out without drawing attention to myself? If they noticed me, a whole band of them would attach itself to me purely out of courtesy. I couldn't even relieve myself without being observed.

I didn't care. I had to do something, or it would kill me. My stomach heaved threateningly. Any moment now, I would disgrace myself.

I managed to shake off my retinue. One of them shouted out after me: "Use the dung heap, that's the closest."

I followed the example of the Roman, though I lacked a peacock feather. O blessed relief!

Luckily, when I returned, the host was in full flow. Not wishing to be outdone by his lordship, his style tended towards the hyperbolic. He alluded rather deftly to Uncle Béla's speech, and the blessings of the Almighty. Then he turned to an appreciation of the late pig. It was quite miraculous how its distinguishing qualities gradually expanded. At this rate, by breakfast time it would boast slabs of back-bacon half a meter long.

It was a fine eulogy. People have an inextinguishable impulse to say something complimentary about those who have been sacrificed for their benefit. How much more dignified, how much more worthy of respect is the behavior of the lion, calmly licking his chops, as if to say: lucky antelope. Now, instead of jumping about uselessly, his flesh and bones will turn into lion.

As we plodded homeward, Uncle Béla recounted the incidents of the evening, chief among them the menu, which surpassed any criticism. I was only half listening, as I inwardly acknowledged and paid my respects to those highly cultured Romans, thanks to whom I had escaped the day's gastronomic adventure in one piece, and, with luck, would now pass an undisturbed night.

I woke the next day with a dull head, but the cool air streaming down from the green, wooded hills soon cleared out the cobwebs.

Otherwise, the days passed, one much like the other. A stroll round the yard and the gardens; making friends with the horses and cows; walks to Királd and in the woods. The dear woman's reedy voice —"Béla, aren't you hungry?"—as she hobbled about. Poor thing, she was always chasing around, to the extent that her frail body allowed, after the maids, who idled about aimlessly. There were six of them now, wasting time and stealing firewood and wheat.

"I had to hire another one, to lighten poor Anna's load."

As far as I could see, this just made the confusion worse, with each one trying to push the work onto the next, while Annuczi rose at five in the morning; she could still be heard at midnight, opening and shutting doors, going from room to room and looking into cupboards and under beds, or outside, searching for her favorite cat and calling its name.

"Fritzi, my darling! Fritzi, my darling!"

He was the nastiest and most amorous tomcat of the lot. He and his beloved yowled away at their love-tryst's hymn with such abandon that, finally, a carter took his revenge by driving a pitchfork right thought him, puncturing him in three places. Annuczi nursed him for a week, to no avail; though he held out long enough for general peace to be restored.

———

In the evenings, by the warm, orange-ish light of the petroleum lamp, Uncle Béla and I would discuss world politics and how the war was going. Not much was changing, or looked likely to change. Everything seemed to have come to a standstill. It was "all quiet on the Western front." This was even more horrible; everyone waited impatiently for something to break the deadlock.

The fighting that ensued involved no movement on either side. The armies were dug in within a few meters of each other. On occasion, troops fraternized with the enemy, especially on the eastern front, and opposing forces even made local truces. The commanders, naturally enough, took a dim view of this, as it undermined the fighting spirit. At any rate, apart from some skirmishing, the fronts had frozen, the lines had become ever more effectively fortified and impregnable, and nuisance fire was wasted into thin air. In general, the fronts had lost much of their initial horror.

True, the Entente's announcements were not encouraging: "Time is on our side"; "The war will be won by the side that has the stronger nerves"; "The war has just begun." The West has yet to mobilize fully. The airplane is the weapon of the future. A lot of reassuring pointers and slogans. The Germans, for their part, held out the prospect of chemical warfare. They had already created a gun that surpassed anything that had gone before: the "thirty-five." Then the forty-two centimeter; whereupon the enemy moved into underground concrete bunkers.

A race had begun between offensive weapons and defenses. The powers had, for the time being, reached equilibrium. But the West's resources, unlike ours, were inexhaustible.

As we debated these things, our positions became increasingly polarized between Uncle Béla's optimism and my pessimism.

"I accept that my position is not based on personal experience. For that very reason, I maintain that I am able to judge the facts more objectively. For you, everything is overshadowed by the traumatic experience that almost ended your life. The deductions you draw can't be objective."

I shrugged my shoulders and held out my arms.

"All right, I can see how that could be argued. But, for the life of me, there's nothing I can do about it; nor can the hundreds of thousands of men like me, who can't escape from the influence of their subjective experience. Armies are made up of young men whose instinct for life makes them fight for survival; reasoning plays no part. Wars used to be decided by individual battles that lasted a day or two. The momentary fervor of youth, fanaticism, or enthusiasm could survive that long.

"I think the West have got it right when they count on nervous exhaustion. Their geographical situation, their wealth and their greater populations will enable them to hold out longer than we can. As I see it, if we haven't won this war within a year, we've lost.

"I see the force in much of what people are saying. But don't forget that, as well as material readiness, you need psychological readiness. I'm not sure that the latter isn't the more important."

We both fell silent. Uncle Béla fiddled with a pellet of bread and gazed off into nothing. I would be sorry to upset him. Oh well. The argument would continue tomorrow, though for my own part I was finding it pointless, and was bored by it.

"Well, I'll say goodnight, Uncle. It's time I went to bed."

"'Night, Bélus. Sleep well."

Sweet dreams.

A door separated his room from mine—an old-fashioned low door with a brass handle and, in the center, a little disc-shaped polished brass knob. I used to hear him still moving about late into the night, or reading by candlelight. The candle often burned out, as he would fall asleep.

Tomorrow would be the first of March. I had to report at the end of the month for a medical examination. Now, as I attempted to weigh up the results of my time here, I concluded that I had imagined it differently. I had thought that I might be able to create some kind of extraterritorial existence for myself, where I could reconnect with my past life, take up the works I had begun but left unfinished, assess the compositions so far just sketched out with a few strokes, shut my eyes and stop my ears.

It was impossible. All that I had thought, imagined, or conceived felt alien, incapable of development. Alien. No longer relevant. Something had been broken inside me; or perhaps in the whole order of the world. Or in everything. For now, there was no way out. Perhaps I should let the past tear itself free from me, and allow myself to be carried by the tumultuous flood tide of the times.

I imagined my father's voice. "Son, you must stop this brooding." I say nothing and look at him. How can I make him understand?

"You're always so pensive. There are deep lines on your forehead that weren't there before."

"There's a lot that wasn't there before. And there's a lot on its way that we know nothing about."

Oh well. Let's get some sleep.

———

I woke early—although there is no such thing as "early" in the country, and there was already movement in the street outside.

The wooden shutters did not close perfectly, and the shaft of light that forced its way though the chink projected an image of the passers-by and carts outside onto the far wall of the room—but in reverse. The fundamental principle of sight and photography. I watched with childlike delight. The sun was up and shining; it was early spring; I had another month of life; and suddenly one word transfixed me: the sea! Maybe for the last time. Maybe there, in Lovrana,[2] where I had been in love. A veritable avalanche of joy hit me. I whistled as I shaved.

Annuczi was there at breakfast.

"Annuczi, my dearest. I've been so happy here, and I want to thank you for everything." However, etcetera. "I'd like to go home tomorrow. They'll be pleased to see how much weight I've put on."

She looked serious.

"We've been so happy to have you here. You know how much Béla loves you, and who knows when we shall see you again?"

Oh, please let us have no goodbyes!

I left Királd railway station at dawn the next day for Eger.[3] Szilvásvárad, Bélapátfalva, Mónosbél . . . places that held happy, sacred memories for me.

Eger, where I had painted the great church at sunset to commemorate the ordination of Uncle Béla's class of candidates for the priesthood. That had been ten years ago, when I still believed in the sanctity of art.

Another world.

12. LOVRANA

My unexpected arrival at home was cause for delight. My father was at the office, but mother could not get her fill of me.

"You've become a new man in these three weeks."

"More's the pity! They'll send me off again."

I tried to be lighthearted. I quickly outlined my plans: if possible, I would be leaving for Lovrana tomorrow. My mother pressed her hands together.

"Still so restless, son! Wouldn't it be good to rest here at home? There's your expensive studio standing idle. Instead of devoting yourself and your time to calm work, you flit about."

I sat hunched despondently in the corner of the divan—my usual place—and racked my brains: How to put into words the rupture that had taken place within me? I knew that, until I found the point at which I could reconnect, I would have no peace.

She stood in front of me.

"You mustn't think that I want to hold you back if you feel that travel will bring you relief. It's just that I feel sorry for you, son. You're in the prime of your life, and you've gone quite gray at the sides. It so saddens your poor father, too." Her voice wavered and became thin.

An hour later, when she came back from the kitchen, I could see that she had taken a firm grip on herself. She smiled and held out a bundle of letters.

"They came while you were away." She watched me attentively. Of the ten letters and postcards, five were letters of between four and eight pages from E—— H——. I put them in my pocket.

"I'll read them all tonight, when things have calmed down."

"You can be so cold and heartless sometimes, I hardly recognize you."

I decided that I would definitely leave by the fast train at six the next day. I did some packing. I went up to the studio. Even the air in there was still, but it was tidy. Teréz had her own key and she strove to justify the fifteen korona I paid her each month. (That, too, annoyed my mother: you pay her for nothing, there's no need for her. We could look after it ourselves.) I found my wonderful set of English watercolors from Winsor & Newton, in their splendid pocket-size enamel box with its water dish, and the block of excellent Fabriano watercolor paper. I had these with me in Taormina,[1] and whenever I looked at them I was seized by the urge to paint.

My father was waiting for me when I got home. I could see that my mother had prepared him. He seemed cheerful.

"You're looking so much better. I hear you're off again tomorrow. Well, live your life, son, while you can."

———

I took the afternoon fast train for Fiume. Not many passengers. I found myself an empty compartment and took the window seat, facing west, with no one to bother me as I settled in. With fifteen minutes to go before departure, I got out and walked up to the engine. A connection with the great love of my lost childhood, its object of fascination and wonder: the steam engine. This was the latest type—the Class In, with its round-nosed boiler, three sets of driving wheels over two meters in diameter, capable of a hundred kilometers an hour. I would watch out during the journey to see how it behaved.

The Eastern Station was more neglected than I had ever seen it. The little park by the departures had disappeared, its lawns trampled to mud. Exhausted-looking groups of soldiers had set up camp on it. Inside the vast hall, listless groups of soldiers loaded up with full packs dragged their feet. A porter shouted "Last platform on the left!" at the top of his voice. The traffic was less than half of what it used to be.

The whistle blew, and I jumped aboard. There were only six carriages, one of them an empty sleeping car. The train soon picked up speed, and I felt a rush of youthful enthusiasm. Here we go, towards the old world of freedom! There wouldn't be many visitors. That would suit me fine. I didn't need company. I needed the mountains, Monte Maggiore,[2] the kindly villagers in the hills, the fishermen on the shore. And the sea. I needed the sea. I needed to sit on the cliffs by the shore, gaze at the waves as they rolled in, and listen to the whispered hiss, or the roar, of the pebbles on the beach; and to be hypnotized by the surges of seafoam washing up the little rocky inlets, whose music Böcklin could still hear, even as death's dry fiddle squeaked in his ear.[3]

I would be staying at the Mausers'. I had already sent a telegram to say I was coming. I might be the only guest. How nice that would be! That charming little villa—a symbol of homeliness, security. and calm. The padrone: sturdy, muscular, and grave, thick hair cut en brosse, the full moustache, a crease between his brows like an exclamation mark, the wrinkled brow—a steadfast, sure, fair-dealing man of forty-six who expected to be dealt with fairly, or else. He had a dairy herd which grazed on the lower slopes of Monte Maggiore, and he supplied the district with milk, as far as Abbazia.[4] He had made a fortune; still, the whole family was up at four every day. *Mama* Mauser sparkled with cleanliness and order, the embodiment of Puritan virtues. She ran the pension. The older daughter worked in the office, and the younger assisted her. The boys attended school. The whole family was an example of kindliness, devotion to duty, and affection: the Germanic family ideal. The younger daughter was very pretty, but unfortunately too young for me.

The conductor came in. I gave him five korona and asked him to make sure I was left in peace, as I wished to get some sleep. He promised to oblige. I stretched out along the seat on one side. Secure and undisturbed in my curtained-off compartment, I daydreamed about Lovrana.

It was still early, and dusk was just starting to fall; but if I was able to get to sleep now, I could wake at dawn and enjoy the magical deep valleys beneath the clouds clinging to the Karst's rocky peaks, the bare mass of cliffs gilded by the blazing orange rays of the rising sun, the bay of Buccari emerging out of lilac mists, as in a dream, a thousand meters below, the blue panorama of distant islands, and the beloved sea.

I awoke at Cameral-Moravice.[5] The conductor was knocking softly at the door. Perfect! A ten-minute wait here while they changed engines. There was hot freshly brewed tea in the station. I had to take advantage of the opportunity. Tea in hand, I went to take a look: a matched pair of my old favorite, Hungary's biggest mountain engine, twelve driven wheels between them to haul the train up to above a thousand meters.

I sat by the window and immersed myself in the beauty of the wakening forest. Here and there, a few late glowworms streaked like shooting stars, then were lost in the darkness of great forests of ferns; there were millions of them here. By the time we got to Lič, the highest point on the line,[6] it was light. The morning mist still obscured the view of the sea, which was visible from here in dry weather. Up here, snow still lay in many of the hollows, and there was condensation on the windows. Now the train began to gather speed, until it rushed headlong downwards through curve after curve, its clattering multiplied to an earsplitting din by the surrounding stone walls. The sunlight streamed down now. Nature was bursting into green. It was already springtime here. O happy day!

The coastal steamer was waiting in its usual place. Nothing had changed here, apart from the absence of crowds and the quiet. Perhaps it only seemed so quiet in comparison with the summer.

The war was far away. Serbia no longer mattered, Italy was our ally, Switzerland was neutral. Goodbye to all of that.

The steamer slid across a calm sea. *Mare olio.*

I gazed in pleasure at the beauty spots along the coast as we passed: Veprinac and Castua; Volosca and Abbazia, where we stopped off; then past Ika; and now here I was. A solitary cab waited at the jetty. I might as well arrive like a gentleman. Actually, I would have done better to get off at Abbazia, as the Mauser was closer to there. No matter. They greeted me warmly. The whole family was there, except for the padrone, who would be home in the evening. Mrs. Mauser, who was about forty-five, was very sweet. The older girl, Miri, was positively bursting with health, if a little to excess. Elsa, the younger one, was very attractive, with eyes that shone with life. For the sake of propriety, they made a point of informing me that she had turned sixteen just the day before. Still, I could see that I was a hit in my splendid double-breasted tunic. I was the only guest. They would bring me breakfast in my room, and I would eat lunch and dinner with them. Daily full board was five korona. I could eat as much as I liked.

So, what was I going to do here? If I was enjoying myself, I would stay to the very last day. It would cost a hundred and fifty korona for the month—half my salary. In fact, I ought to stay. I could go up onto the slopes of Monte Maggiore with *papa* Mauser and his herd and paint figures, animals, and landscapes, like the great Segantini.[7] I would make my haunt the *lungomare*—the winding, zigzag coastal path that runs from Abbazia to Moschiena.[8] Then there was the mountain; I might take a boat trip to Fianona; and I would draw and paint. The urge to work was bounding inside me.

I didn't see *papa* Mauser until the evening. He paused in the doorway. There was not a flicker of movement in his face, which might have been carved in stone. He bowed his head deeply, then turned on his heel.

We had finished dinner, but at the request of the family I spent the rest of the evening with them. Elsa played the piano, very nicely. A delightful child. Then I was required to give an account of my experiences on the battlefield—not an easy task with my German, but we managed. They reacted with ingenuous horror, moderated by courtesy and consideration. Elsa gazed at the "hero" in fascination. Afterwards, we played a card game called *schwarzer Peter* for matchsticks. It was my first evening of gaiety and happiness in six months. My room on the first floor opened onto the sea; lulled by its rhythmical sound, I slept splendidly.

The rumble of thunder woke me in the gray half-light. The breeze blowing in through my open window was unexpectedly warm; the sea was in tumult. I waited impatiently for the daylight. I was going to paint waves.

This, I was informed over breakfast, was the *Sirocco*, and there would be a swell of three to four meters.

I headed off in the direction of Moschiena. In many places, the *lungomare* was awash, and I had to climb up to the coastal road which ran parallel to it. At Moschiena, a stream flowing down from Monte Maggiore had formed a shallow bay, some five hundred meters across. Here, I observed the marvelous spectacle of perfect waves being formed. So gripped was I by their beauty that I realized at once that there would be no painting. A rocky spur stood out darkly among the pebbles, and I watched wave after wave as they crashed against and surged over it. I wanted to keep watching until the physical principles that governed them, their form, and the colors that appeared in them became ingrained in me. From all of these similar but never identical waves I hoped to be able to abstract *the* wave.

That evening, whenever I shut my eyes, row upon row of waves rushed towards me, like old friends. Let there be one more day of these Titans storming ashore. I would definitely start painting. I went to bed at peace with myself, and felt as I were being rocked to sleep.

I was impatient to finish breakfast: the roar from outside urged me on. From the sound of it, the *Sirocco* was raging with full force.

Only now did I realize just how far I had wandered yesterday. I found the spot where I had been sitting, and the rock that jutted out into the water. Less of it showed today, as the tide was in. But the waves were just as big as the day before—that was the main thing. Ready to jump out of the way, I watched intently as they broke. I had it now. Feverishly, I set to work; soon, the external world ceased to exist for me.

If the rock on which I was sitting had not been quite so hard, I might have lost all track of time. I had to struggle to get to my feet. I had done it: surely, the best wave that I had ever drawn.

I was filled with happiness. The war had ceased to exist. There was quiet, there was peace; I was alone, and nature scattered her beauty before me. All I had to do was pick it up and present it to mankind, in all his folly.

A glance at my watch reminded me: you must hurry back for lunch with your kind hosts and tell them what a happy morning you've spent. Elsa will fix her eyes upon you and play you some Chopin.

I got home out of breath, just in time. I showed them the watercolor as evidence, to squeals of delight. As well as Chopin, Elsa played the Moonlight Sonata for me. Ah, Beethoven: the heroes' hero.

I withdrew to the privacy of my room in a state of reverie. By the time I awoke, the sun was on its way down. I wanted to relive the happiness of that morning in solitude. There were some abandoned formal gardens, of great age, up above the old town in Lovrana, with cypresses and great chestnut trees. The old pathways were marked by the occasional mossy stone step and the barely discernible remnants of former buildings. Resting my head on a moss-covered rock, I enjoyed the distant view to Cherso and beyond.

Would I ever again have a day of such blessings?

———

The *lungomare* became my constant haunt. My favorite stretch was in the direction of Moschiena. The coastline here was precipitous, undercut by the waves with little chambers, which were refuges of silence. The sea, seemingly still, lapped the little coves with a visible slow swell, disturbing the pebbles into a soft murmur, then slapping up against the vertical cliff face with a snap, like the end of a whip. Sitting on a stone washed smooth over millennia, I painted one of the caverns. Forms and colors beyond reckoning. A lifetime would be too short to exhaust the eight-kilometer stretch between Lovrana and Moschiena. An inexhaustible fount of beauty, yet this was but the merest crumb, the tiniest fragment of the universe.

In the evening, we played the usual session of *schwarzer Peter*. A slightly imbecilic game, but it was a balm to my nerves to be together with these straightforward, decent, honest people.

I made drawings of the members of the family—the two girls and the two boys. I started with Elsa, but drew the others as well, so as to avoid any awkwardness. Her eyes shone and her face was aflame. If only she weren't such a child!

I crossed over to Fiume as well. I had planned to walk as far as Volosca on my way back, but the path did not hold out much promise. I turned back and sat on a stone bollard on the dockside to wait for the ship. That unfamiliar silence again. Three smartly-dressed Italian men hurried past, gesticulating energetically. They huddled together as they spoke, or rather gabbled, using not just their heads but their shoulders, their arms, even their knees. These people's temperament always seems to border on agitation.

The ship slowly swayed. Few passengers. Soporific silence. I was startled awake by someone racing past in front of me, waving. The same scene ashore, with a different cast.

That evening, Mauser appeared suddenly at the door. His face immobile, he beckoned *Mutti* over. He bent his head close and spoke to her. She spread her arms, then sat down again to our card game, her face serious. I could see that there was something she could not keep to herself, and would sooner or later have to blurt out. So it proved. She laid her cards down carefully and leaned in to me.

"They're saying that Italy's getting ready to leave the Triple Alliance. Things could become very difficult for us here."[9]

I swallowed hard. I did my best to explain matters in a way that would calm their fears. I could see that they hung on my every word.

I'm a soldier, so I must know what I'm talking about.

I had seen Italian soldiers mobilizing at the time of the Italo-Turkish War.[10] Women threw themselves in front of troop trains to stop them leaving the station. Men wept and wailed; carabinieri ran about yelling. These people were not soldiers. Austria could deal with them with one arm behind its back.[11] Still, it gave one pause.

Had it all caught up with me even here?

We went on playing *schwarzer Peter* in silence, but no one was paying it any attention.

All of a sudden, some terrible animal fear burst upon me, and everything abound me span. The lid on the cast-iron stove clattered rhythmically, the pictures danced on the walls, and the lamp that hung from the ceiling swayed. From outside came a thundering sound as if some huge set of steel shutters had been yanked down. I felt as if the floor were sinking beneath my feet.

I sprang up. Frightened eyes stared glassily at me.

"*Erdbeben,*" announced Miri. "*Hoffentlich es ist schon vorbei.*"[12]

My knees were trembling as I sat down. They made me drink some cognac and saw me up to my room. They did all they could to calm me down. This had happened before. Fortunately, it had caused no real damage, not so much as a cracked chimney so far.

Miri confessed that, until now, she had not believed that there was anything the matter with me, as I looked so well. But now she knew that I really was ill.

I was to ring the bell if I felt unwell in the night.

I felt dreadfully ashamed at having lost my self-control, and I tried to demonstrate that I was perfectly all right. But when they left me to myself, I spread wet towels over my heart and lay like that, fully dressed, on top of the bed. It took hours before I calmed down; but I didn't undress, thinking that if it came again, I would run down to the shore.

Thus did I live through my first and, I hope, last earthquake. The sum of my feelings was, quite distinctly, one of utter doom.

How calmly I had observed the spectacle of Messina in ruins from the earthquake![13] It's one thing to see, or read, or hear about something. It's another to live through it.

———

The next day, I received a telegram from Ervin Voit, informing me that he had managed to get some time off work—no easy matter, apparently—and that he would be coming down to Lovrana for a week at Easter. I was to see about a room for him.

I was genuinely delighted to hear this. So many shared joys, shared enthusiasms, and feelings bound us together in friendship. The remnants of yesterday's drama were swept away, almost as if it had never happened.

He arrived tired out. His wan face looked almost waxy, his elegantly slim frame somewhat stooped; but with his fair curled beard and quiet voice, he nevertheless presented a distinguished and attractive gentlemanly figure. I could tell that this was the impression he made on the family when I introduced him. His decorative appearance did not go unnoticed—especially by the girls.

He was delighted with his room, next door to mine, and looking out over the sea.

"Here, at last, I can relax," he declared, eyeing the broad divan. "I got practically no sleep on the train. There was a full moon, and the scenery was simply stunning."

I told him that I ate with the family, and it would look anti-social if we altered that arrangement.

For a moment, he looked taken aback, as if anxious that the independence which he had so painfully lost by getting married, so yearned for, and had—if only briefly—now regained, was in danger.

"Of course—if that's what they'd rather."

"I'll leave you to get some rest. You can have lunch when you wake up."

The family were touched that Ervin also wished to eat with them, if we were happy with that arrangement. He promised to learn how to play cards—something he had never done in his life.

It was late afternoon by the time he reappeared, refreshed after sleep and unrumpled. He declined all offers of a full lunch, saying he just wanted a bite to eat. The quantities of chocolate, whipped cream, fresh butter, jam, honey, and various cheeses that this involved put a normal lunch to shame.

He was eager for a walk by the seashore before it started to get dark. We set off on the *lungomare* towards Abbazia, where I was familiar with every cliff, cavity, and inlet.

We sauntered along, stopping here and there to marvel at the sea, which he, too, loved. With his softly spoken, quiet nature, I didn't wish to disturb his rapt state of contentment. Why speak at times like this?

Beauty. Peace. Happiness.

We walked as far as Ika. One side of the little cove was occupied by a trattoria, with little tables set out among the flowering oleander. We shared a half liter of *vino rosso* and gazed off into the distance lost in blue mist, where the glowing sky kissed the glittering water's mirror.

"You've done some beautiful things since you've been here. That wave is especially good. It must have taken courage to resolve something like that, to that degree, using watercolor."

I won't deny that his recognition gratified me.

"I'm amazed that, after what you've been through, you can focus your will onto a subject that's so difficult to observe. Nature remains the source of all beauty, the sole cure for whatever ails the body and the mind."

"Look, I've been at the stage many times now where I felt that something in me had snapped, that I'd lost the connection with the old me, and like someone groping about in the dark, I couldn't find the thread that would lead me out of a pitch-black mine. Now, for the first time, I've felt some sort of glimmering of light within me, the possibility of a way out, by turning to nature. But not in the way that I used to, in a generalizing sort of way, but rather with the kind of reverence with which Szinyei immersed himself in the beauty of a freshly ploughed patch of earth, the varying forms of its gleaming clods and its colors. I've escaped back into nature, and I feel I've made the right choice.

"I've wondered whether this unprecedented catastrophe that's hit the world can make the human creative spirit more productive. Will it inspire some magnificent dramatic theme? After all, it produces tragedies by the minute, and heroic, or grandiose, events and incidents. More's the pity. The official war artists have churned out every kind of allegorical celebration of heroism. There may be all sorts of reasons for this, but perhaps it's not just the artists who are at fault. War itself has lost whatever glory it might once have had. It's lice and guts-ache."

"I follow you," said Ervin. "I agree with all you say, and I'm glad to hear that you've found a way forward. Where I think you may go slightly wrong is to blame everything on the war. Artistic anarchy was already wreaking havoc before the war started. Remember the exhibition by 'The Eight'? I don't get that Béla, either." Béla Bartók[14] was Ervin's cousin. "Before coming here, I attended a little concert of his. You can imagine what I felt—me, whose ideal is Chopin. I thought I was going to tear myself apart in agitation. It would start in harmony, and I would begin to relax and give myself up to the music; and then suddenly one of the violins would slice into it with a dissonant squeal, like a sharp knife. Then, all of a sudden, they stopped. The end, but without an ending. At least I could stop holding my breath. The Jewish kids went wild. Most of the audience just stared at each other in bewilderment."

He shook his head and took a gulp of *vino rosso*.

"Well, the twentieth century hasn't made a terribly encouraging start."

We sipped at the wine for a bit.

"You know," I said, "if one frets about these things, one starts to feel as if one had got caught up in some great tangled ball of thread. The more one struggles with it, the worse the tangle, and there's no unraveling it. Slogans chase each other round and round: 'renewal,' 'youth forward,' 'new vision,' 'democracy,' 'impressionism,' 'naturalism'—a whirlwind of 'isms,' one succeeding the other, faster and faster. Each one serves only to heighten the confusion. Some revolutionary transformation may already be under way; or this may all just be straws in the wind.

"A year ago, at the school, a cheeky little Jewish girl stopped me and asked: 'Sir, what do you think of Benczúr?' I gave her a frosty look. 'Why do you ask?' 'Because when we feel like a joke, someone says "Benczúr," and then we all have a good laugh.' I gave her a stony stare for her effrontery, then I waved her aside, as if to say 'get lost.' But you know, she may not have been entirely to blame. I think it's this poisonous spirit that's spreading far and wide, like a miasma of swamp gas.

"Who benefits from this wrecking? What's the purpose of it? A lot of people associate it with the socialist revolution that's smoldering away—look at how the left and its newspapers behaved in relation to the outcry over 'The Eight.'

"I hate the wrecking and the destruction of things. Especially when I have nothing better to put in their place. That's why I loathe war, and loathe destruction of any kind, even if it's wrapped up as part of some well-intentioned revolution.

"I hate injustice and the hurting of defenseless creatures. I'm not a weakling—you felt my muscles in Novi—and I'm not a coward. Remember when I gave that cabman in Rottenbiller Street a beating that night? He was thrashing that horse, tortured half to death, with the whip handle. On its head, its nose, its eyes. I told him to stop hurting the poor exhausted creature. He came at me with the whip. I left him lying on the ground."

Ervin felt my arm. "Yes. You're pretty much back in shape, and you're combative enough. You were born for the front."

I waved him aside and went on.

"On my way home, I rather regretted losing my temper, mainly because I realized that he'd only take it out on the wretched horse. But that poor defenseless victim meant more to me than its beast of an owner."

Dusk was falling. The pink glow spreading up into the sky from the west played on one side of the waves, green shadows on the other.

"I enjoy listening to you. I agree with you one hundred percent, though I suspect that may be partly the *vino rosso*."

Slowly, we got up and started back towards Lovrana.

I broke the silence. "Listen, I feel like I did after taking confession, back in the days when I was a devout little boy. I have that same feeling of inner peace. Though I must admit it's stirred things up inside me as well.

"I don't suppose that you've come here to wrestle with the world's problems, any more than I have. We're both here to devote ourselves, with no distractions, to whatever peaceful joys and beauties this earthly paradise can offer. Let's talk about those, or not, but let's not speak any more about war, and the things that go with it. Let's go straight up to Castua tomorrow."

The weather had favored us with a glorious day. Ervin reported that, back home, people were still squishing about through slush. Here, spring was unfolding in all its splendor.

From Abbazia, we made our rattling, swaying way on a tram, accompanied by squealing and grinding noises, to the oil refinery.[15] This was beautiful too; here, even this had its charm.

Finding one's bearings from the shore was simple. The mountains rose before us, dotted with smaller or larger settlements—a sort of bird's-eye view in reverse. Veprinac on its hilltop, like something in a fairy tale. To the east of it, Castua. From afar, it looked like a mediaeval fortified settlement. We had a two-hundred-meter hill to climb. It was bare, with the shriveled remains of fig trees here and there, and farmhouses overgrown with vines that had never been pruned. Kitchen gardens, no bigger than a room, surrounded by stone walls; the soil in them gathered together by the basket load from deserted houses, rotten tree stumps, and gullies. Tiny fields of wheat on a little plateau. Stunted rye and oats, which they harvest with sickles and tie into wreaths, like flowers.

A Hungarian peasant would sit and weep.

And yet, these were big-boned, heavy, sinewy people, with a somehow lordly presence and urbane manners. But from what? The Mausers believed that it was the sea. They were sailors, fishermen, and sometimes workmen.

Cheerfully, we plodded upwards. We crossed the railway line from Fiume. The blessed sun was almost scorching. We were climbing in our shirtsleeves. Beside the railways tracks, a railwayman, assisted by a mechanic, was spreading pitch onto his cape, spread out on the ground, to render it waterproof. It did not bear thinking about that he might actually wear it—hopefully, once it had dried, although this was uncertain.

Passing the ruins of former buildings, we were greeted by a chorus of croaks, crunks, and crepitations. We reached an abandoned open cistern. This was the source of the concert: innumerable toads the size of side plates gamboled about here, full of the heady joys of spring. Yellowish (*terra di Siena*), with yellow-green markings, they splashed about among the floating weeds in the muddy green stagnant water. The larger males squatted on the backs of the females, one human-looking foreleg embracing the female's neck, croaking love's sweet song. The weeds were woven through and through with strings of tiny balls the size of peppercorns.

We continued on upwards. When we started to flag, we would sit on a limestone rock, its surface weathered to a rasp, and gaze out over the magnificent panorama. We could not get our fill of its beauty. Then we would press on for another stretch.

"It's beautiful all right, but imagine having to do this perhaps several times a day!"

We approached Castua. A little mediaeval Italian town with its piazza and its *duomo*. The place had evidently seen better days. The pieces of meat hanging in the smelly little *macelleria* were black with flies, legions of them greenly glinting. We searched for a trattoria, and found one. But neither of us liked the look of it. I had my suspicions about the *frutta di mare* and suchlike.

Now that we had got here, it seemed only right to make a sketch. I drew, while Ervin lay on his back, softly whistling the intermezzo from *Cavalleria rusticana*.[16]

It was dark by the time we got home, tired but happy. We met Mauser in front of the house. He was in a hurry to leave, and his "good evening" was crisp and stiff.

"Is he always this formal?"

"He's a thoroughly decent chap, but I've never seen him smile."

That evening, Miri told us that the master had brought serious news about the moves that the Italians were making. It thoroughly spoiled the good mood I had been in. *Post equitem sedet atra cura.*[17]

———

We visited Tersatto, a castle above Fiume. The Croatian guide explained that it had belonged to the *famiglia Frankopana*. He spoke Hungarian with poor pronunciation, but comprehensibly: a believer in the friendship between Croats and Hungarians, or maybe it was just for our benefit. We parted on friendly terms. We called out: "*Živio!*"[18] He replied: "Hurrah!"

We continued wandering around the ruins on our own. Eventually I found a detail for a drawing—a little staircase through an archway, fragments of an old ruined tower. The lighting gave it a decorative effect. It would have suited a stage set for some Italian opera.

Ervin had found a subject a little further off, and I could hear him cheerfully whistling *Cavalleria rusticana*.

We strolled back along the *lungomare*. Neither of us spoke. The sea had settled down to sleep; at long intervals, a smooth wave lapped against the rocks. We did not meet another soul the whole way home. The friendly warm ochre light of its windows beckoned.

I had kept getting delicately reproachful glances from sweet little Elsa for spending all my time with Ervin since his arrival. I hadn't played cards with her or asked her to play the piano; instead, tired out, I had been going straight to bed.

Well, now it was her turn. Even the usually reserved Ervin charmed them. We asked Elsa to play some Chopin. She played as if in a state of rapture, quite beautifully. Ervin listened, his head bent forward, and wiped tears from his eyes.[19] I felt that I loved these people. It was not a good thing to be this happy in the present situation, for it brought with it thoughts of paradise lost.

—

We had also planned a trip over to Novi, to bring back the memories of our last carefree summer. However, it was not possible to accomplish this in a single day, and we didn't fancy spending a night somewhere unfamiliar. We only got as far as Fiume-Sušak, but this was a very pleasant trip. The weather continued to favor us, and on the way home the sunset was so magnificent that we couldn't take our eyes off the sea. Before us, the sun's rays shining through the rising and falling waves ranged from turquoise to Mitis green, through ultramarine, to the deepest Prussian blue. The waves' crests shone in shades of pale violet—almost white—and cerulean blue. When one

turned around, the setting sun bathed everything in purples, or-
anges, and glowing pinks. It was unforgettably beautiful.

In the course of our daily wanderings, we still came across some
ancient Italian street life in the little streets that clung to the Fiume
hillside, but the shore and the port appeared to be almost devoid of
life. This had a very depressing effect on us.

"It's the war that's caused it."

"Was it already like this when you arrived? There are rumors in
Budapest about the Italians."

"Here too. To have to escape from here as well would really be all
I need. I decided that I was going to try to avoid even thinking about
the war, but now that it's come up, what's the mood like in Budapest?"

"Well, everyone's getting sick of it. Nobody really believes the official announcements any more.

"Both sides are reinforcing their positions. One side comes up
with a new weapon, the other side comes up with a defense against
it. There are torpedo boats to launch torpedoes, there are destroyers
to sink the torpedo boats, there'll probably be destroyer-destroyers
to sink the destroyers, and so on.

"Both sides talk about 'final victory,' and both struggle for peace
against the war that each has forced on the other.

"The grand statements don't really have any effect any more.
Everyone's become completely impervious to them. Which means
they've got away with it. I used to stick little flags into the map I had
pinned on the wall so that I could follow the movements on the
various fronts. I've given up on all that.

"There's no trace now of the romantically enthusiastic send-offs
from the start of the war. The problems of everyday life—so far,
hardly noticeable—are starting to press to the fore. And, let's be
honest, everyone's starting to pay more attention to the matter of
their own security than to matters of war and peace. It's only among
the older people now that you still find enthusiasm and hope. There's
nothing, really, at stake for them. They feel relatively secure, and
they have the time for it.

"Sadly, this was inevitable. It's natural when the passing of time brings no decisive results. This is, in fact, 'total' war, which directly affects ever greater masses of people.

"I think the longer it lasts, the worse it'll be for us. We'll be more and more shut in, and we won't be able to take it economically. And all this is nothing compared with what still awaits us.

"Let's not sigh yet. It'll make no difference anyway. Let's look at the sea and think about how we'd paint it."

———

It was time for Ervin to leave for home. I had decided to stay on until Easter, which was approaching. After that, I would return home and spend the time that remained until I had to report for duty there.

I saw Ervin off to the steamer; we parted on the understanding that there would be no goodbyes. We had had enough of those. Life—in whatever manner—would go on. We were young, and we wanted to live. To surrender to lethargy was to be lost. One senses one's destiny, but one can influence it by one's will. So we parted cheerfully: "Until the next time! It's been fun. We'll do it again as soon as we can."

I attended Easter mass with the Mauser girls at the little church, an intimate chapel in the Italian style. The locals sang as only Italians can. There was a festive lunch of every imaginable delicacy. I slipped away afterwards to my beloved abandoned old park, and caught myself paying it a farewell visit. I stroked the sappy, moist trunks of the cedars and cypresses, I gazed at the panoramic view, and as I ambled homeward I began to turn my mind to thoughts of packing. I would be leaving the day after tomorrow. How these three weeks of happiness had flown by!

It was time to say goodbye—or rather, to part. I thanked them sincerely for all they had done to lift me up from my fallen state. *Mama* Mauser was moved to tears. So, a little, was I.

"*Auf Wiedersehen am nächsten Winter. Im Weihnachten ist hier auch sehr schön.*"[20]

I promised that I would.

I had to rise early, as my train left Fiume in the morning. But the whole family had beaten me to it. I left the drawings I had done of the girls as a memento, and I had ordered two huge bouquets of roses, one for each day that I had spent with them: red ones for Elsa, white ones for Miri. They put them in their windows, from where they waved to me as long as they could still see anything of my departing cab.

Auf Wiedersehen.

I stood by the window all the way up to Lič. From here, a thousand meters up, I caught one last glimpse of the panorama of islands lost in cobalt blue and violet, and the endless sea.

Auf Wiedersehen.

———

The train raced down the northern slopes of the Karst, hammering down through long curves, between stone walls, and among dense forest, thickets of fern, ravines, and rushing mountain streams. The landscape became bleaker, and it got colder. Snow still lay in the depressions of the burnt sienna, russet, and ochre moorland. In the deep course of a stream, the water ran between banks covered in snow and ice, pale green and scummy. Here and there, among the great bluish-gray trunks of beech trees, flashed the occasional vivid green, mossy trunk of a Turkey oak.

Apart from the rushing of the train, there was silence. The few passengers spread themselves out, taking their pick of window seats facing in the direction of travel. No one spoke.

At Cameral-Moravice, the giant Karst engine was replaced with a fast big-wheeled engine. There was time to get out and have a cup of coffee. It was chilly; I'd got used to the spring. I decided to travel the remainder of the journey in the restaurant car.

We tore along through flat country now. A cheerless landscape: gray mud in the sloping road that ran alongside the tracks, the ruts in it half a meter deep. Poor horses! Not a human being to be seen anywhere. What could they do out there in the mud?

Zagreb: another change of engine. Bolhás, Kaposvár, Dombovár,

Simontornya, Rétszilas... names that meant nothing, whose magic came only from their association with the sea.

I bought a newspaper. I had not read one for weeks. Bellicose guff about final victory. The big German offensive towards Paris had "stopped" at the Marne.[21] No decisive developments anywhere.

Slow dusk.

Budapest.

EPILOGUE

DRÁFI, the gypsy drummer, was a short, bandy-legged little chap. Whenever he saw me, he would salute and grin at the same time—contrary to regulations, but radiating goodwill.

Once or twice I called him over.

"Look, you're not supposed to grin when you salute."

A look of uncertainty and fear flickered in his eyes; then, seeing that I was smiling too, he once more beamed from ear to ear.

"All right. Don't forget now!"

While we were waiting at Komárom,[1] on our way to the front, he asked permission to get off the train. I asked him what for.

"Wish to report, sir, my family's here."

A horde of gypsy children raced towards him with wide open arms. All had bare potbellies and all were barefoot. Their skin was a magnificent reddish brown. After them came a gypsy woman in a headscarf and brightly colored skirts, her gnarled hands pressed to her mouth. Then they fell upon each other, and their tears flowed without words.

Afterwards, back on the train, he trotted up and down amongst us during the endless days and endless nights as we headed northeast.

After we left Rava Ruska, we rested at the edge of the Dabrovka forest, beside a freshly ploughed potato field. A few paces from me, Dráfi was scrabbling about in the grass. He had a mate with him, one of the reservists. I stepped over.

"What are you up to, Dráfi?"

He was about to jump to his feet to report, when the mate spoke up.

"Sir, he's found a potato. He wants to plant it in the ground."

"It's got such good shoots. It wants to live. I'm going to plant it. It might live longer than me."

Poor Dráfi.

The potato did indeed outlive Drummer János Dráfi of the Royal Hungarian Army.

Béla Zombory-Moldován, *The Wave*, Lovrana, 1929. Watercolor.

The subject and composition correspond with the drawing described in Chapter 12, but this is a later work, evidently re-creating the (presumably, lost) drawing of 1915 on a post-war return visit to Lovrana.

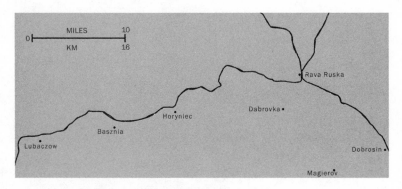

Rava Ruska and its vicinity, showing railway lines in 1914

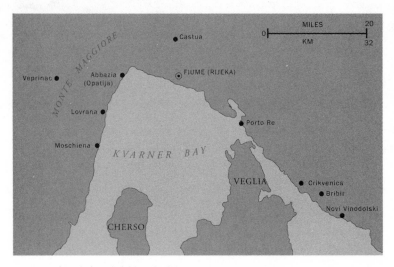

Fiume (Rijeka) and the head of the Kvarner Bay in 1914

NOTES

NOVI

1. An ancient Croatian hill town a few kilometers inland from Novi.

2. Austria-Hungary declared war on Serbia at midday on Tuesday, July 28, 1914. Public news of this probably reached Novi on July 29, with notices calling up reservists as part of mobilization against Serbia posted the same day. BZM had six days to report for duty in Veszprém, in western Hungary, with a recently formed infantry regiment of the Royal Hungarian Army (*Magyar Királyi Honvédség*, literally "Hungarian Royal Homeland Defense Force"—abbreviated to *Honvéd*).

3. Hungary had risen in revolt against Austrian rule in 1848—"the year of revolutions." Although the rebellion was crushed, it signaled the revival of Hungarian nationhood.

4. Zsigmond Sebők (1861–1916), Hungarian journalist and writer of children's literature. He edited the children's magazine called *Jó Pajtás* (Good Pal), produced by the Franklin publishing house, for which BZM drew illustrations.

5. 1882–1932; Hungarian painter and graphic artist and friend and colleague of BZM at the Budapest School of Applied Arts, where he taught costume design.

6. Novi Vinodolski is one of several picturesque towns on the section of northern Adriatic coastline belonging to pre-1919 Croatia. With the connection of Fiume (Rijeka) to the railway network in 1873, this area attracted genteel summer visitors from all over Austria-Hungary. Croatia-Slavonia, though part of the Kingdom of Hungary, enjoyed a degree of self-government. Trieste, Istria, and Dalmatia were provinces of Austria.

7. The sailors are, presumably, Croats, on their way to Austria-Hungary's naval base at Pola. Their song satirizes the Hungarians.

8. 1859–1929; Hungarian journalist and writer. He co-edited *Jó Pajtás* with Zsigmond Sebők.

9. Cherso (Cres), Veglia (Krk), Arbe (Rab), and Lussino (Lošinj) are islands off the Istrian coast, famous as beauty spots. It is presumably one of these that Gustav Aschenbach, at the beginning of Thomas Mann's *Death in Venice*, finds uncongenial and abandons for Venice.

10. The Eight (*A Nyolcak*) was a group of avant-garde Hungarian painters, formed in 1909 and influenced by fauvism, cubism, and expressionism. Its members were Róbert Berény (1887–1953), Dezső Czigány (1883–1937), Béla Czóbel (1883–1976), Károly Kernstok (1873–1940), Ödön Márffy (1878–1959), Dezső (Desiderius) Orbán (1884–1986), Bertalan Pór (1880–1964), and Lajos Tihanyi (1885–1938). The group's 1911 exhibition in Budapest created a sensation and sharply divided critical opinion.

11. Kraljevica, Croatia.

12. Now the Croatian city of Rijeka, Fiume was Hungary's seaport until 1918 and the maritime outlet for the eastern part of the Austro-Hungarian Empire.

13. A strong winter wind in the eastern Adriatic.

BUDAPEST AT WAR

1. The express service covered the 502 kilometers between the two cities in under twelve hours.

2. BZM had served as a "one-year volunteer" in 1909 (instead of doing the normal two or—in the common army—three years of compulsory military service) after completion of his studies at the Hungarian Academy of Fine Arts. One-year volunteers had to meet an educational requirement and pay for their own clothing, food, and equipment. At the end of their year, they passed into the reserve. Those like BZM who subsequently passed a qualifying examination received an officer's commission with the rank of ensign in the reserve.

3. The chorus of a jingoistic song of this title ("Megállj, megállj, kutya Szerbia!"), which enjoyed great popularity in the first weeks of the war.

4. "Toreador, love awaits you!" From the "Toreador's Song" in Bizet's *Carmen*.

5. In fact, his stepmother. BZM's mother died in 1895.

6. From a ribald folk song.

7. 1885–1954; Hungarian painter and graphic artist.

8. 1872–?; Hungarian painter.

9. 1885–1924; Hungarian painter.

10. 1870–1911; Hungarian painter.

11. The Nagykörút (Great Ring Road), built in 1896, is a grand semicircular boulevard around the center of Pest, modelled on the famous Ringstrasse in Vienna.

12. This is probably Friday, July 31, 1914, when both Russia and Austria-Hungary declared general mobilization; a state of readiness for imminent war (*Kriegsgefahrzustand*) was proclaimed in Germany; and a German ultimatum was sent to Russia. The risk that Austria-Hungary's war on Serbia might trigger a continental war thus became a virtual certainty. The newspaper in front of whose offices—next door to the famous New York Café—the scene takes place was probably *Az Est* (Evening).

13. 1882–?; Hungarian painter.

14. 1884–1949; Hungarian painter.

15. The Hungarian Academy of Fine Arts, where BZM studied from 1903 to 1908. He refers to it by a student nickname of the day, *a Tökéria* (the Perfectery)—a play on the institution's founding mission "to contribute to the perfecting of every branch of the nation's fine arts."

16. *Fészek* means "nest." This was one of the coffeehouses frequented by artists and critics; from about 1916, it became a haunt of radicals and the literary avant-garde. Not to be confused with the artists' club of the same name, of which BZM was a leading member.

17. Probably the Hungarian painter Sándor Teplánszky (1886–1944).

18. 1860–1931; Hungarian painter.

VESZPRÉM

1. A historic city in western Hungary, close to the eastern end of Lake Balaton.

2. The *Ausgleich* (Compromise) of 1867 established the dual monarchy of Austria-Hungary as a union between the Austrian Empire and the Kingdom of Hungary under a head of state who was both emperor of Austria and king of Hungary. Accordingly, at a ceremony in St. Matthias Church, Budapest, on June 8, 1867, Emperor Franz Joseph I was crowned king of Hungary by the Hungarian prime minister, Count Andrássy, and Archbishop Simor of Esztergom. Franz Joseph's consort, the Empress Elisabeth of Bohemia, was crowned queen by Bishop Ranolder.

3. An early indication, perhaps, of the resort to the printing presses to meet the enormous costs of the war. The amount of paper money in circulation doubled between July 1914 and December 1915, fueling inflation.

4. Istvan Medgyaszay (1877–1959) was a Hungarian architect, noted for his use of motifs from Hungarian folk art on buildings in the idiom of the Vienna *Sezession*.

5. 1845–1914. A leading and prolific exponent of the *Sezession* style of architecture in Hungary. Many of his designs incorporate brightly colored tiling inspired by folk art.

6. A traditional Hungarian spirit, typically distilled from apricot, plum, or pear. Its alcohol content can be up to seventy-five percent by volume.

7. A high-security prison in an old fortress in northern Slovakia, notorious for the harshness of its regime.

8. Hungarian was the language of command in the Royal Hungarian Army. The other junior officers, including BZM, had presumably done their military service in the "common" army of the monarchy—the *kaiserliches und königliches* ("*k.u.k.*") *Heer*, or Imperial and Royal Army—in which the language of command was German.

9. An order of chivalry founded during the First Crusade.

10. "It is a comfort to the wretched to have companions in misery." The Latin proverb's probable origin in the *History of the Peloponnesian War* of Thucydides (book VII, chapter 75) makes it seem particularly apt.

11. Ferenc Pogány (1888–1946); member of the Royal Hungarian opera company 1912–1926. He was taken prisoner by the Russians and held in captivity until 1920. He was, in fact, a baritone.

12. József (Joseph) Diskay (1889–1960); member of the Royal Hungarian opera company. He emigrated to the USA in 1919 and pursued a career in Hollywood.

13. A town at the western end of Lake Balaton.

THE MARCH

1. The first verse of a traditional Hungarian folk song.

DEPLOYMENT

1. 1848, i.e., the Hungarian revolt against Austrian rule.

2. An Austrian possession from 1772, Galicia extended north and east from the Carpathian Mountains to the Austro-Hungarian Empire's long border with Russia. This strategically important territory, with Lemberg (L'viv) as provincial capital and a major military stronghold at Przemysl, saw a succession of titanic clashes between four Austro-Hungarian and five Russian armies from the opening days of the war until 1916. After a tentative initial advance into Russian territory, Austro-Hungarian troops fell back but won the Battle of Zamosc-Komarów (August 26 to September 2, 1914). However, the decisive engagement of this first phase of the Galician campaign was the Battle of Rava Ruska, which began on September 6, 1914. BZM's regiment, the Veszprém 31st Honvéd Infantry (of the 41st Honvéd Infantry Division of the Third Army), was in the thick of the battle; having already suffered heavy losses, it now needed urgent replenishment.

INTO THE FIRE

1. The German and Polish spelling is Rawa Ruska (sometimes Rawa-Russka); now Rava-Rus'ka, Ukraine, close to the border with Poland. In 1914 the town was twenty-four kilometers from the Russian border.

BZM's unit probably arrived there on September 7, 1914, the second day of the battle, in which some 300,000 troops were engaged along a ten-kilometer sector of the front.

2.   Dabrovka (Dubrivka) is about five kilometers south of Rava Ruska.

3.   Once it had acquired range, a battery of field artillery would lay down concentrated fire to "sweep" a given target area. The other side's reserve troops would be held what was considered a safe distance outside that area until required in the front line, but remained vulnerable to "nuisance fire."

4.   Austro-Hungarian military doctrine required infantry to advance line abreast in "firing lines" (*Schwarmlinien*).

5.   The Steyr-Mannlicher M1895 rifle was the standard infantry weapon of the Austro-Hungarian army in World War I.

6.   The distinctive standard knapsack (*Tornister*) issued to Austro-Hungarian troops had a pony-skin or cowhide front flap.

7.   Legislation to increase military expenditure and enlarge and re-equip the army introduced in the Hungarian parliament in 1910 was held up for two years by the nationalist opposition, who demanded the introduction of Magyar as the language of command in Hungarian units of the common army and equality of Hungarian with Austrian flags and insignia.

8.   From the aria "E lucevan le stelle" in Puccini's *Tosca*, sung by Cavaradossi as he awaits execution.

9.   Kassa (Košice), the second largest city in Slovakia. The lower ranks of the 34th "common army" infantry regiment, which was based there, were preponderantly Slovaks.

10.   Artillery shells packed with steel or lead balls, which are projected forward when a small charge at the base of the shell explodes near the end of the shell's trajectory.

11.   A type of artillery shell first used in World War I. Unlike a shrapnel shell, it contains a powerful explosive, bursting the entire shell into fragments propelled in all directions with great force.

12.   The villages of Magierov (Maheriv) and Dobrosin (Dobrosyn) are

about ten kilometers apart and roughly fifteen kilometers to the south and southeast, respectively, of Rava Ruska. The main front during the battle had run roughly north-south through this area.

13. A general retreat of the Austro-Hungarian First, Second, Third, and Fourth Armies from Galicia to the Carpathian Mountains—a distance of over a hundred kilometers—was ordered late on September 11, 1914, when the Russians threatened to encircle the Second, Third, and Fourth Armies from the north and the Germans declined to come to their aid.

14. This was putting it mildly. Austro-Hungarian casualties in the war's disastrous first two weeks totalled 400,000 men, including 100,000 taken prisoner by the Russians. The regular officer class was virtually wiped out. Russia lost 250,000 men, of whom 40,000 were taken prisoner.

15. The "castle" is probably the Poniński palace in Horyniec (now Horyniec-Zdrój, Poland), some eighteen kilometers southwest of Rava Ruska. The building survives as a sanatorium.

BACK TO LIFE

1. Lubaczow lies some seventeen kilometers west of Horyniec.

2. Ruthene (Rusyn) would be intelligible to a speaker of Slovak.

3. This Jewish shtetl cannot be identified with certainty, but might be the village of Wulka (Wólka) Horyniecka. Its entire population would be among the approximately 434,500 Jews murdered between March and December 1942 at the Nazi extermination camp at Belzec, about twenty-five kilometers to the north.

4. BZM writes that the name was "something that sounded like 'Rammia,'" but it can confidently be identified as Basznia (Basznia Dolna), which lies approximately midway between Horyniec and Lubaczow and is the only stop on the railway line between those two places. The unmetalled direct track from Horyniec joins the road at this point.

5. Consciously or otherwise, BZM seems to be paraphrasing (or parodying) Théodore Géricault's celebrated painting *The Raft of the Medusa*.

6. A rusty-purplish artist's pigment.

7. Now Nowy Sącz, in southern Poland.

8. "Hail, Caesar; those about to die salute you." Quoted by Suetonius in *The Lives of the Caesars* and attributed to prisoners condemned to die in mock battle before the Roman emperor Claudius. BZM may also have in mind a painting of the subject by Jean-Léon Gérôme.

9. The highest mountain range in the Carpathian Mountains, and the natural border between Galicia and Slovakia (then part of the Kingdom of Hungary).

10. Now Prešov, in Slovakia.

11. Now Košice, in Slovakia.

12. In eastern Hungary.

13. "What is natural is not dirty." From the Roman writer Servius's commentaries on Virgil's *Georgics*; perhaps a bookish reference to Jóska's peasant background.

14. BZM uses a contemporary expression which translates literally as "coffeehouse Conrads," after Franz Conrad von Hötzendorf, chief of the general staff of the Austro-Hungarian armed forces until 1917.

15. Endre Ady (1877–1919), prominent and controversial Hungarian poet and journalist, associated from 1908 with the reformist literary journal *Nyugat* (West). Ady attracted a devoted circle of followers; many conservatives regarded him as a self-indulgent egotist and betrayer of his homeland.

16. József Egry (1883–1951); Hungarian artist; a modernist. BZM calls him "Egri" (a familiar Hungarian surname), but this appears to be a misspelling.

17. 1880–1941; Hungarian sculptor.

18. Probably Péter Gémes-Gindert (1876–1923), Hungarian sculptor.

19. An important artists' colony in Pest which flourished in the 1890s and continued during the early decades of the twentieth century.

20. Gyula Benczúr (1844–1920); Hungarian painter and pedagogue. An influential traditionalist.

21. József Mányai (1875–?); Hungarian painter.

22. 1874–1950; Hungarian painter.

23. 1884–?; Hungarian painter.

24. "How are you?" in Slovak.

25. A traditional Slovak spirit distilled from juniper berries.

26. This is not standard Slovak, but may be a dialect survival from Old Slavic, meaning, literally, "(of) the high-born lady." The English equivalent might be "your ladyship."

HOME AGAIN

1. 1889–1948; Hungarian graphic artist and caricaturist.

2. 1882–1937; Hungarian poet and journalist.

THE HOSPITAL

1. Possibly a version of the popular song "*Jaj, de szépen muzsikálnak*" (Oh, how beautifully they play), of which at least two gramophone recordings were on sale at the time.

2. 1884–1950; Hungarian graphic artist, architect, and stage designer.

3. "Traumatic neurosis" was a controversial diagnosis described by the German neurologist Hermann Oppenheim (1858–1919), who attributed post-traumatic nervous symptoms to supposed physical changes in the brain caused by fright. The theory was discredited after 1918. BZM's symptoms would now be regarded as classic indicators of post-traumatic stress disorder.

4. The First Battle of the Masurian Lakes ended on September 15, 1914 with the defeat of the Russian First Army in East Prussia. If BZM's recollection of this as the occasion for the celebrations is accurate, they seem to have been at least a week after the event: he cannot have entered the hospital before about September 18.

5. The opening line of the elegiac poem *Mohács* by the Hungarian dramatist Károly Kisfaludy (1788–1830). The poem's subject is the disastrous

Battle of Mohács of 1526, at which the Ottoman Turks defeated the Hungarians, bringing an end to Hungary's independence for four centuries. The second line of the poem apostrophizes the battle as the "graveyard of our nation's greatness."

LEAVE

1. Count István Tisza (1861–1918) was prime minister of Hungary (for the second time) from 1913 to 1917. "Pista" is the familiar abbreviation of "István."

2. BZM taught at the Budapest School of Applied Arts, where he was principal from 1935 to 1946.

3. 1876–1925; Hungarian actress.

4. Lajos Ágotai (1861–?).

5. A line from the "outlaw's song," of which BZM sings the first verse in chapter 2.

6. A colossal monument to the 1813 Battle of Leipzig, completed in 1913.

7. A popular and sentimental *opéra comique* by Ambroise Thomas, first performed in 1866.

8. Count István Széchenyi (1791–1860); a leading liberal politician, theorist, and writer, he was an influential advocate of the modernization of Hungarian society.

9. 1885–1972; Hungarian sculptor.

10. 1812–1905. The Chain Bridge opened in 1849.

11. BZM occupied an apartment in this building (no longer standing), during the 1920s. It took its name from the sixteenth-century tomb of Gül Baba, poet and companion of Sultan Suleiman the Magnificent, which then stood in its grounds.

12. 1870–1932; Hungarian painter.

13. Ferenc Márton (1884–1940); Hungarian painter and sculptor.

14. 1883–1914; Hungarian sculptor. He was killed in battle on October 2, 1914 in the Uzsok Pass in the Carpathians.

15. István Lipót Gách (1880–1962); Hungarian sculptor and painter. He was taken prisoner by the Russians and held (in Tashkent) until 1920.

16. A village approximately 120 kilometers northeast of Budapest, close to the modern-day border between Hungary and Slovakia, now incorporated into the town of Ózd. BZM's uncle, Béla Zombory, was the Roman Catholic prebendary there from 1912.

SAJÓVÁRKONY

1. BZM was promoted to the rank of second lieutenant on November 4, 1914.

2. Now Lovran, Croatia. Situated on the western coast of the Kvarner Bay in the northern Adriatic, the town was a fashionable resort in the years before World War I, when it was territorially part of Austria.

3. A historic city in what is now northern Hungary.

LOVRANA

1. BZM visited the fashionable Sicilian resort in 1912.

2. The Italian name of the mountain range that rises behind the western coast of the Istrian Peninsula.

3. Arnold Böcklin (1827–1901); Swiss painter. The allusion is to a self-portrait in which the artist is accompanied by the figure of Death playing a violin; and probably to *Villa by the Sea* (of which Böcklin painted several versions), depicting waves breaking onto a rocky Mediterranean shore.

4. Now Opatija; a resort about six kilometers north of Lovrana on the Istrian coast.

5. Now Moravice, Croatia; from here, the Budapest-Fiume railway line ascends steeply up to the Karst plateau, for which a mountain engine would be required.

6. The highest point on the line is, in fact, the Sleme tunnel, at 879 meters. Lič, where the sea comes into sight, is at 811 meters.

7. 1858–1899; Italian painter, celebrated in his day for visionary depictions of pastoral life in the high Alps.

8. Now Mošćenička, Croatia; a hill town about six kilometers south of Lovrana on the Istrian coast.

9. The Triple Alliance of Germany, Austria-Hungary, and Italy dated from 1882, but Italy's enthusiasm for it waned; she did not enter the war in 1914, but started secret negotiations with Britain, France, and Russia to switch sides in exchange for a promise of territorial gains at Austria's expense. Agreement was reached on April 26, 1915 and Italy declared war on Austria-Hungary on May 23, 1915.

10. 1911–1912. Italy invaded and seized the Ottoman Turkish provinces of Tripolitania and Cyrenaica (modern-day Libya) in a costly and inept war.

11. This was a widely held view in Austria-Hungary at the time. Events, of course, proved otherwise. The fighting on the Italian front from May 1915 to November 1918 was bitter, largely static, and bloody even by the standards of World War I.

12. "Earthquake. Hopefully, it's over."

13. A massive earthquake on December 28, 1908, flattened the Sicilian city of Messina and triggered an enormous tsunami. Over 120,000 died.

14. 1881–1945.The piece that Voit describes may be Bartók's String Quartet No. 1 in A minor, completed in 1909.

15. When it opened in 1883, the oil refinery at Fiume was the largest and most advanced installation of its kind in Europe. Financed by the Rothschilds in Vienna, it processed crude oil from the Baku oilfields in Russia (later, from neutral Romania) and supplied Austro-Hungary with petroleum products.

16. The first Hungarian production of Pietro Mascagni's one-act opera was conducted by Gustav Mahler, then resident conductor at the Budapest Opera, in 1890, six months after its Italian premiere. Ervin's choice is curiously appropriate: the action of the opera takes place at Easter in the main square of a Sicilian village, to which the young Turiddu has just returned from military service.

17. "Behind the rider sits dark Care." The source is Horace's *Odes*. BZM may have known the bronze relief of the subject by the British sculptor Alfred Gilbert.

18. Literally, "may [he/it] live!"; used in Croatian as a toast ("cheers!") or an exclamation of approbation ("hurrah!"). The guide replies with the Hungarian *Éljen!*, which has the same literal meaning, but is used only in the latter sense.

19. A drawing by Voit entitled *Chopin Sonata* depicts a scene uncannily like the one described here. It was published in 1909.

20. "See you next winter. It's lovely here at Christmas, too."

21. The Battle of the Marne (September 5–12, 1914) ended with the retreat of German forces to the river Aisne, some sixty-five kilometers to the north, where they dug in. Germany's strategy of a quick victory in the West was in ruins; four years of trench warfare ensued.

EPILOGUE

1. A city on the river Danube, now on the Hungarian-Slovak border; a major railway junction in 1914.

OTHER NEW YORK REVIEW CLASSICS

For a complete list of titles, visit www.nyrb.com or write to:
Catalog Requests, NYRB, 435 Hudson Street, New York, NY 10014

* *Also available as an electronic book.*